THE RIDGEWAY
NATIONAL TRAIL

About the Author

Steve Davison is a freelance writer and photographer who has lived in Berkshire for over 20 years. He has written several guidebooks as well as articles for a number of outdoor magazines and national and local newspapers, specialising in hill walking as well as UK and European travel, with interests in nature, geology and the countryside. A keen hill walker for many years and holder of a Mountain Leader Certificate, Steve has also worked as a part-time outdoor education instructor. He is a member of the Outdoor Writers and Photographers Guild. Find out more about him out at www.steve-davison.co.uk.

Other Cicerone guides by the author
Walking in the Thames Valley
Walking in the New Forest

THE RIDGEWAY NATIONAL TRAIL

by Steve Davison

2 POLICE SQUARE, MILNTHORPE, CUMBRIA LA7 7PY
www.cicerone.co.uk

© Steve Davison 2013
First edition 2013
ISBN: 978 1 85284 694 7

Printed by KHL Printing, Singapore.

A catalogue record for this book is available from the British Library.

All photographs are by the author unless otherwise stated.

Acknowledgements

The author would like to thank Jos Joslin, National Trails Manager for the Ridgeway, for her help in checking the accuracy of parts of this guide.

Advice to Readers

While every effort is made by our authors to ensure the accuracy of guidebooks as they go to print, changes can occur during the lifetime of an edition. If we know of any, there will be an Updates tab on this book's page on the Cicerone website (www.cicerone.co.uk), so please check before planning your trip. We also advise that you check information about such things as transport, accommodation and shops locally. Even rights of way can be altered over time. We are always grateful for information about any discrepancies between a guidebook and the facts on the ground, sent by email to info@cicerone.co.uk or by post to Cicerone, 2 Police Square, Milnthorpe LA7 7PY, United Kingdom.

Front cover: The view north-east towards Whitehorse Hill, with Uffington Castle on the horizon (W–E Stage 3; E–W Stage 10).

CONTENTS

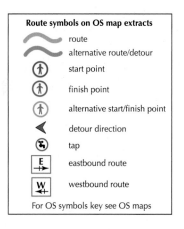

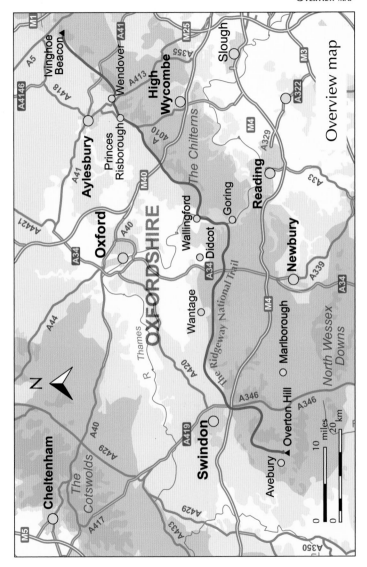

Overview map

The Ridgeway follows the broad grassy outline of Smeathe's Ridge down towards Ogbourne St George (W–E Stage 1; E–W Stage 12)

INTRODUCTION

Walking the Ridgeway National Trail takes you on a journey through a landscape steeped in history, following old trackways that have been used since prehistoric times past the remains of Neolithic burial mounds and Iron Age hill forts with commanding views. On the way there are plenty of distractions just off the route, from picturesque towns and villages with thatched cottages and cosy pubs, to historic churches and interesting museums.

The Ridgeway has been here for thousands of years, so take your time and enjoy the journey. Rest a while and listen: high above the skylarks sing, far off a church bell rings, the wind rustles through the trees, sweeping views stretch out over the rounded chalk hills with wide open skies. Imagine the travellers that have been this way before, where were they going and why. Whether you do one continuous walk, or prefer to spread the pleasure over weeks or years, you'll never forget your journey along the Ridgeway.

As for describing the Ridgeway, maybe that is best left to local naturalist Richard Jefferies in his book *Wildlife in a Southern County* (1879):

A broad green track runs for many a long, long mile across the downs, now following the ridges, now winding past at the foot of a grassy slope, then stretching away through a cornfield and fallow. It is distinct from the wagon-tracks which cross it here and there, for these are local only, and, if traced up, land the wayfarer presently in a maze of fields, or end abruptly in the rickyard of a lone farmhouse. It is distinct from the hard roads of modern construction which also at wide intervals cross its course, dusty and glaringly white in the sunshine...it runs like a green ribbon...

PLANTS AND WILDLIFE

The Ridgeway meanders through a patchwork of open chalk grassland, broadleaved woodland and farmland. Below the downs, chalk streams flow from the spring-line, which forms along the boundary between the upper porous chalk and a lower impervious layer of clay, which results in water that has seeped through the porous layer being forced to the surface. Chalk streams support a diversity of plant and animal life: some of these streams, known as winterbournes, are seasonal and only appear during the wetter winter months. The richly wooded character of the Chiltern Hills distinguishes them from other, commonly more open, chalk landscapes such as the Marlborough and Berkshire Downs. Many of these

(clockwise from top left): British Bluebell (hyacinthoides non-scripta); Cowslip (primula veris); Clustered Bellflower (campanula glomerata); Common Spotted Orchid (dactylorhiza fuchsii)

woodlands are known as ancient woodlands, having been continuously wooded since at least 1600. These areas tend to support a greater number of species and their character often closely reflects the underlying soil conditions, producing a wide range of woodland types and wildlife habitats.

You should have plenty of opportunities for catching glimpses of local wildlife, from foxes to roe and fallow deer or the much smaller muntjac: you may even catch sight of the elusive badger as dusk approaches, or an edible dormouse around Tring Park. Alongside the River Thames you may see the vivid turquoise-blue and orange flash of a kingfisher as it darts along the river, while the ever-present ducks and mute swans will keep you company.

In the ancient broadleaved beech and oak woodlands you may hear the drumming knock of the great spotted woodpecker declaring its territory, or the raucous call of a jay, while in late spring and early summer many of the woods are carpeted with vivid bluebells. The open chalk grasslands support a myriad of butterflies, plants including gentians and orchids, as well as traditional farmland birds such as the colourful pheasant and yellowhammer or flocks of redwing and fieldfare feeding on autumn berries. High above you might see the majestic silhouette of a buzzard or hear the high-pitched whistling call

Small Heath Butterfly (coenonympha pamphilus)

– 'weeoo-wee-weewee' – of a red kite: buzzards have broader wings and a rounded tail, red kites have a distinctive forked tail and chestnut-red plumage. Red kites were successfully re-introduced between 1989 and 1994 and their numbers have steadily increased: you'd be unlucky not to see one, especially along the eastern half of the Ridgeway.

GEOLOGY

The geology of the Ridgeway and surrounding area tells the story of the seas that once covered southern England and the sediments that were laid down between 105 and 65 million years ago. It is perhaps easiest to think of the geological structure as a multi-layered 'cake'. At the base are the oldest rocks – the Gault Clays and

Red Kite (milvus milvus) above Lewknor

Upper Greensand – which date from the Lower Cretaceous (145–99 million years ago). Next is a thick (220m) layer of Upper Cretaceous chalk (99–65 million years ago), mainly composed of the tiny fossil skeletons of a type of algae called coccoliths. Finally at the top are the more recent layers, such as the Reading Beds, London Clay and Bagshot Sands.

During the Palaeogene period (65–23 million years ago) the collision of the European and African continental plates – an event that formed the Alps – caused the 'cake' to ripple, with a gentle tilt to the southeast. More recently, erosive forces have cut through the layers to reveal the underlying geology.

The exposed upper edge of the chalk layer forms a prominent ridge with a steep north-facing scarp slope along the edge of the Marlborough and Berkshire Downs to the River Thames at Goring, and then continues along the Chilterns. To the north lie the wide, flat plains of the Vale of White Horse and the Vale of Aylesbury. This layer of chalk passes south under the Kennet Valley and reappears to form the North Hampshire Downs, as well as the Purbeck Hills in Dorset and the North and South Downs, which include the White Cliffs of Dover in Kent.

Associated with the chalk are irregular silica concretions, known as flints, which also occur in profusion in the jumbled deposits of weathered chalk known as 'clay-with-flints'. Being a very hard-wearing rock, flint has been widely used as a building material and is a characteristic of the region: when struck, flint breaks with a shell-shaped fracture, leaving very sharp edges, and Stone Age man used flints to make hand axes and arrowheads.

The Manger below Whitehorse Hill – a great example of a coombe or dry valley (W–E Stage 3; E–W Stage 10)

A natural process of patchy and irregular hardening within the sandy beds produces boulders of tough sandstone, which appear on the surface when the softer sands are eroded. These are the famous sarsens, known locally as Grey Wethers – from a distance they are said to resemble sheep (a 'wether' is a castrated ram). Sarsens were used in the construction of the stone circle at Avebury and the Neolithic long barrows at West Kennet and Wayland's Smithy, and can be seen lying in the fields at Fyfield Down National Nature Reserve and around Ashdown House.

More recently, glaciation has played its part, despite the fact that the ice sheet never extended south of the line of the River Thames. The deep, sinuous dry valleys, or coombes, that can be seen along the chalk scarp, such as The Manger at Whitehorse Hill and

Incombe Hole near Ivinghoe Beacon, were carved by rivers during the last Ice Age when the usually porous ground was frozen. Another dramatic feature was the creation of the Goring Gap and the diversion of the Thames southwards to flow past Reading: originally the river flowed through the Vale of St Albans, past Watford and Hertford. The gap was created when a large glacial lake, which formed over the Oxford area, eroded a line of weakness in the chalk.

WHEN TO WALK

Walking the Ridgeway can be undertaken at any time of the year. However, if you are walking the full length over the space of a week or two, then between early spring and the end of autumn is probably best, offering the chance of more

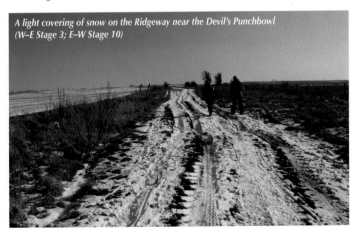

A light covering of snow on the Ridgeway near the Devil's Punchbowl (W–E Stage 3; E–W Stage 10)

settled weather and better walking conditions.

Spring and early summer are great for wild flowers, including carpets of bluebells, especially in the Chilterns, whereas cooler autumn nights herald a dramatic change, with the trees becoming clothed in spectacular shades of russet, gold and brown. Winter days are much shorter, but a frosty or snowy winter's day on the Ridgeway can be a magical experience.

Fortunately, seasonal restrictions that apply during the wetter months from October to April have reduced the damage done to parts of the Ridgeway by eliminating motorised vehicles (except farmers' vehicles). Furthermore, in 2006 parts of the Ridgeway were reclassified as Restricted Byways, which are closed to recreational motorised vehicles.

Both of these measures have resulted in improved walking conditions, especially during the winter months.

PLANNING YOUR WALK

The Ridgeway may only be 139km (87 miles), and pass over comparatively gentle terrain; however, for your own enjoyment and convenience you need to plan your visit carefully in advance. In this guide the route has been split into multiple shorter stages so that you can decide how far you would like to walk each day, whether you are walking the Ridgeway over the space of six days or are doing one or two stages at a time.

For anyone wishing to walk the Ridgeway in six days, a typical schedule would be:

- Day 1: Overton Hill to Ogbourne St George (14.6km/9 miles)

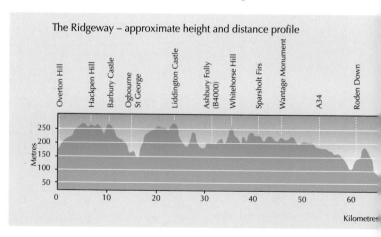

The Ridgeway – approximate height and distance profile

- Day 2: Ogbourne St George to Court Hill Centre (31km/19¼ miles)
- Day 3: Court Hill Centre to Streatley (22.5km/14 miles)
- Day 4: Streatley to Watlington (24.5km/15¼ miles)
- Day 5: Watlington to Wendover (27.8km/17¼ miles)
- Day 6: Wendover to Ivinghoe Beacon (18.5km/11½ miles).

However, this is quite a demanding schedule and you must bear in mind that accommodation is mostly off the Ridgeway, meaning that the day's distance will be longer than just walking the trail itself. An eight-day schedule would include a mix of short and long days, giving time to enjoy the sights along the way, whereas for those wishing to spend more time exploring the surrounding area using some of the detours provided, then 10 or 12 days may be a better target. The choice as to how long you take is yours based on your experience and preferences.

GETTING TO AND FROM THE RIDGEWAY

Swindon railway station, which is on the main line from London Paddington to Bristol and South Wales, is located 21km (13 miles) by road to the north of Overton Hill, with regular daily bus services from Swindon to Devizes/ Trowbridge via Avebury. Pewsey railway station, on the line from London Paddington to the south-west, is located 15km (9½ miles) by road to the south of Overton Hill, with bus links via Marlborough to West Overton and Avebury (except Sundays).

At Ivinghoe Beacon either retrace the route back to Tring rail station

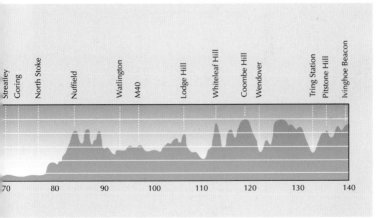

Looking north-north-east from Pitstone Hill to Steps Hill (straight ahead) and Ivinghoe Beacon (left) – the end of the Ridgeway (W–E Stage 12; E–W Stage 1)

(5.7km/3½ miles) for train services on the line from London Euston, or head for Ivinghoe, where there are bus services to Aylesbury and Luton (except Sundays).

There are a number of intermediate railway stations along the Ridgeway, although most of these are located along the eastern section: Didcot (12km/7½ miles); Goring and Streatley (800m – located halfway along the Ridgeway); Cholsey (3.6km/2¼ miles); Saunderton (3.3km/2 miles); Princes Risborough (800m); Monks Risborough (2.3km/1½ miles); Little Kimble (1.6km/1 mile); Wendover (100m); and Tring Station (on route).

Many of the towns and villages located near to the Ridgeway offer some form of bus service, however these can be irregular, liable to change and most do not operate on Sundays. Public transport information may be accessed by contacting Traveline (0871 2002233,

Sundial on the side of the Church of St Mary the Virgin in North Stoke (W–E Stage 6; E–W Stage 7)

www.traveline.info) or National Rail enquiries (08457 484950: www.nationalrail.co.uk). The National Trail website (www.nationaltrail.co.uk/ridgeway) also provides a very useful travel planner with links to bus and train timetables.

For anyone wishing to drive, there are a number of car parks at various locations along the Ridgeway (these are mentioned in the route text) as well as in nearby villages. Always remember to park considerately and be aware that theft from parked cars can occur, therefore do not leave anything valuable in your car.

WHERE TO STAY

Accommodation ranges from campsites and youth hostels to B&Bs, pubs with rooms and hotels; however, these are mostly situated in nearby towns and villages and will involve detours from the trail. Your daily walking schedule and availability of accommodation will ultimately dictate where you stay; places where accommodation may be available are mentioned at the start of each section.

Up-to-date details on accommodation is available from the National Trail website at www.nationaltrail.co.uk/ridgeway or from local tourist information offices (see Appendix B), and a list of accommodation near to the trail is given in Appendix D.

Regarding 'wild' camping, the latest word from the National Trail office is that the land over which the Ridgeway travels is privately owned and the public right of way along it is for passage only, not for stopping and camping. In practice, however, most landowners, when asked, would let you pitch a tent on the trail for a night, as long as you ensure that it disappears the next morning, and that no litter is left, no damage done and no camp fires lit. Do not camp in adjoining fields or woods without prior permission from the landowner.

FOOD AND DRINK

Places where refreshments and food may be available (pubs, cafés and shops) are mentioned in each section, in Appendix C and on the National Trail website: most of these (all of them on the western part) involve a detour from the route and there is no guarantee that they will be open when required. There are also a number of water taps located along the route (details in text). Always ensure you carry enough food and water with you.

WAYMARKING, ACCESS AND RIGHTS OF WAY

The Ridgeway National Trail is well signposted throughout with fingerpost signs – some giving walking distances to various locations – marker posts and National Trail acorn symbols on fences and gateposts: there are also generalised route maps at various locations. The descriptions in this

Ridgeway signage shows the National Trail acorn symbol

guide, along with the map extracts and the signage on the ground, mean that route finding should not cause any problems; however, it is recommended to also carry either the Harvey's Ridgeway National Trail Map or the relevant Ordnance Survey Explorer map, especially for excursions from the main route.

The Ridgeway follows official rights of way, whether that is footpaths, bridleways, restricted byways or byways. Some sections also pass areas of open access land (marked on OS Explorer maps) where you can freely roam.

Rights of way are:
- Footpaths – Yellow Arrow – walkers only
- Bridleways – Blue Arrow – walkers, cyclists and horse riders
- Restricted Byways – Purple Arrow – walkers, cyclists, horse riders and carriage drivers
- Byways – Red Arrow – same as for a byway plus motorcycles and motorised vehicles

USING THIS GUIDE

The descriptions in this guidebook all follow the same format. The information box gives the stage start and finish location accompanied by grid references, stage distance (km/miles), cumulative distance (km/miles), time (hours), relevant map details and details of places close to the route that offer refreshments (pubs, cafés and shops), public transport links and accommodation.

A short introduction gives a brief guide to the stage, identifying any major points of interest, including towns and villages. Throughout the route text you will find various, easily identifiable items or places of interest highlighted in bold type: for the places of interest, additional information is given.

The second part of the guide details route directions for anyone wishing to complete the Ridgeway in a westerly direction, by starting

Nuffield Place – former home of William Morris (aka Lord Nuffield)
(W–E Stage 7; E–W Stage 6)

at Ivinghoe Beacon and finishing at Overton Hill. For practical information and details about sights along the route refer to the corresponding stages in the west-to-east description.

Times and distances

The distances quoted in the text, metric first, with approximate imperial conversions rounded to the nearest ¼, ½, ¾ or whole number, have been measured from OS Explorer maps: note that the heights quoted on the maps are in metres and the grid lines are spaced at intervals of 1km. The walking time for each stage has been worked out using a walking speed of 3.2–4km/hour (2–2½ miles/hour), plus 10 minutes for every 100m of ascent, resulting in a given time of, for example, 4–5 hours for stage 1. This should be treated as the minimum amount of walking time required to undertake

the walk and does not include any time for rests, photography, consulting the map or guidebook, or simply admiring the view – all of which can add substantially to the day's activity.

Harvey Maps produce the Ridgeway National Trail Map, a 1:40,000 (2.5cm to 1km) scale waterproof map covering the entire route and all but a few of the short detours described in this guide. The map is also good for anyone cycling or riding the Ridgeway as it shows both the Swan's Way and Icknield Way Riders Route, which need to be followed for the eastern section after crossing the River Thames.

The Ordnance Survey offer two series of maps: the 1:50,000 (2cm to 1km) Landranger series and the considerably more detailed 1:25,000 (4cm to 1km) Explorer series. The OS maps covering the Ridgeway are:

- Landranger: 165, 173, 174, and 175
- Explorer: 157, 170, 171, and 181.

This guide contains extracts of the Ordnance Survey 1:50,000 Landranger series of maps with overlays showing the route, along with any detours.

The grid references given in the guide are generated from the National Grid. Each map is overlaid by a grid with a spacing of 1km. A grid reference is made up of two letters, which correspond to the 100,000 metre square in which the grid reference lies, and six numbers. The first two numbers correspond to the vertical line (known as 'eastings') to the left of the point of interest: the third number is the tenths of the square (equivalent to 100m). The fourth and fifth numbers locate the horizontal line ('northings') below the point of interest, and the last digit is again the number of tenths moving up through the square. Always remember – the horizontal numbers come before the vertical ones.

CYCLING AND RIDING THE RIDGEWAY

The western half of the Ridgeway, from Overton Hill to the River Thames at Goring, a distance of

Horse riders on Fox Hill (both cyclists and horse riders are allowed to use the Ridgeway from Overton Hill to Goring) (W–E Stage 2; E–W Stage 11)

68.4km (42½ miles), follows bridle-ways, restricted byways, byways and roads that may be used by cyclists (on mountain bikes) and horse riders. Parts of the Ridgeway to the east of the River Thames follow public foot-paths and may not be used by either cyclists or horse riders.

An alternative would be to follow part of the 105km (65-mile) Swan's Way for 32km (20 miles) from Goring (SU 600 807) to Hempton Wainhill (SP 770 012), the bridle route uti-lises both minor roads and bridleway between Goring to Salcey Forest in Northamptonshire. The Swan's Way follows the Ridgeway for 2.5km (1½ miles) from Cleeve Road in Goring to South Stoke (SU 598 836) and then again for 13.7km (8½ miles)

St Andrew's Church in Chinnor has a stunning collection of brasses (W–E Stage 8; E–W Stage 5)

from Britwell Hill (SU 677 920) to Hempton Wainhill (SP 770 012).

From Hempton Wainhill fol-low the 39km (24-mile) Icknield Way Riders Route along bridleways and minor roads to reach Pitstone Hill car park (SP 955 149), which is only 2.4km (1½ miles) from Ivinghoe Beacon. Cyclists and horse riders are not allowed along the final section of the Ridgeway up to Ivinghoe Beacon, as the route is footpath only.

Shortly after Hempton Wainhill the Icknield Way leaves the Ridgeway to follow the Upper Icknield Way to the Wycombe Road via Shootacre Lane, Picts Lane and Poppy Road, rejoining the Ridgeway at SP 805 025 for a short distance before heading through Whiteleaf. Once over Whiteleaf Hill the route passes Chequers to reach Little Hampden and then heads northwards through Dunsmore. At Wendover the route follows the Wendover bypass into Bacombe Lane, and then east along Hale Lane before rejoining the Ridgeway near The Crong (SP 904 085). Once through Tring Park the route leaves the Ridgeway and goes through Wigginton before head-ing north-east to cross the Grand Union Canal and then north past the Bridgewater monument to finish at Pitstone Hill car park.

THE RIDGEWAY ONLINE

For up-to-date information about the Ridgeway National Trail, including transport and accommodation, visit the National Trails website at www.nationaltrail.co.uk/ridgeway. After completing your walk please take time to complete the Ridgeway feedback form available from the National Trails website: this allows the National Trail team to pick up on things that people either have a problem with or would like provided; plus, when you complete the form, they'll send you a certificate and/or a cloth badge.

THE GREATER RIDGEWAY

Running diagonally across southern England, from the south coast in Dorset to the Norfolk coastline, the Greater Ridgeway offers a much more challenging long-distance route. This 583km (363-mile) route follows four distinct long-distance paths:

1. The Wessex Ridgeway – covering 219km (136 miles) from the Dorset coast at Lyme Regis to Marlborough in Wiltshire. Route marking: waymarks with an image of a Wyvern, a two-legged dragon associated with the ancient kingdom of Wessex (www.dorsetforyou.com/wessexridgeway).

2. The Ridgeway National Trail – covered in this guide.

3. Icknield Way – running for 206km (128 miles) from Ivinghoe Beacon to Knettishall Heath near Thetford; there is also an additional multi-user section (Icknield Way Riders Route) from Bledlow that runs parallel to the Ridgeway. Route marking: waymarks with an image of a Neolithic stone axe (www.icknieldwaypath.co.uk).

4. Peddars Way National Trail – the Greater Ridgeway follows part of this national trail northwards for 79km (49 miles) through Norfolk from Knettishall Heath to the coast at Hunstanton. Route marking: National Trail acorn (www.nationaltrail.co.uk/peddarsway).

THE COUNTRYSIDE CODE

As you travel the Ridgeway, please respect the countryside and follow the Countryside Code:

- be safe – plan ahead and follow any signs
- leave gates and property as you find them
- protect plants and animals, and take your litter home
- keep dogs under close control
- consider other people.

Finally, always take care when crossing roads.

THE RIDGEWAY
West to East: Overton Hill to Ivinghoe Beacon

*The view to the east towards Lacey Green windmill from Lodge Hill
(W–E Stage 9; E–W Stage 4)*

STAGE 1

Overton Hill (Avebury) to Ogbourne St George

Start	Overton Hill car park on the A4 (SU 118 680), or the Red Lion in Avebury on the A4361 (SU 101 699)
Finish	Junction of the Ridgeway and a minor road (SU 192 746) near Ogbourne St George, or Ogbourne St George village
Distance	14.6km (9 miles); cumulative 14.6km (9 miles)
Time	4–5 hours
Height gain	200m
Maps	OS Landranger 173; OS Explorer 157; Harvey Ridgeway National Trail Map
Refreshments	Pubs at Avebury, Beckhampton, West Overton, Winterbourne Monkton, Winterbourne Bassett, Broad Hinton and Ogbourne St George; shop and café at Avebury
Public transport	Bus – Avebury to Swindon (trains), Devizes and Marlborough; Ogbourne St George to Swindon (trains), Marlborough and Salisbury (trains)
Accommodation	Avebury, West Kennett, Winterbourne Monkton, Ogbourne St George

The official start of the Ridgeway, at Overton Hill, is not very inspiring – being just a car park beside the rather busy A4 with a track heading north out across the rolling Marlborough Downs. Soon a short detour leads to the fascinating sarsen-strewn fields of Fyfield Down National Nature Reserve. However, the Ridgeway continues northwards, passing the Hackpen White Horse hill figure, to reach Barbury Castle, the first of several Iron Age hill forts along the Ridgeway. After admiring the extensive views the route heads south-east along Smeathe's Ridge before dropping down to Ogbourne St George, where there is a choice of accommodation and a pub.

For anyone interested in exploring Avebury along with Silbury Hill, West Kennet Long Barrow and The Sanctuary before starting the Ridgeway from Overton Hill, it is well worth taking the option of the alternative start from Avebury, which adds 5.2km (3¼ miles).

Alternative start

From The Red Lion (01672 539266) – the 400-year-old inn is claimed to be haunted by the ghost of Florrie, a

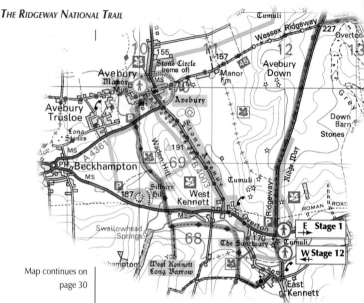

Map continues on
page 30

former
landlady who was mur-
dered and thrown down the well by her husband for
being unfaithful – in **Avebury** (SU 101 699) follow the
High Street south-west past the village shop and soon
turn left along the enclosed path; a small gate on the
left gives access to the stone circle and a track on the
right gives access to Avebury Manor and the Alexander
Keiller Museum and café. To visit St James' Church
(which, although altered by the Normans, still retains its
tall Anglo-Saxon nave), continue along the High Street.

The most impressive feature at **Avebury** is the large
'henge' (a 'henge' is a type of Neolithic earthwork
consisting of a circular or oval bank and ditch) dating from 2600BC. Within this structure is the outer
stone circle, one of Europe's largest stone circles,
originally marked with 98 sarsen stones along with
two smaller stone circles, and part of the present
village. Along with Stonehenge, the Avebury

Part of the stone circle in Avebury

henge and associated sites have been designated a UNESCO World Heritage Site.

The Alexander Keiller Museum is named after Alexander Keiller (1889–1955), heir to the Dundee-based marmalade business, who was responsible for excavating many of the sites at Avebury in the 1930s (the museum houses archaeological finds from the area). Nearby is the Manor House, once the home of Alexander Keiller, which dates from the 16th century (01672 539250; www.nationaltrust.org.uk/avebury).

Keep ahead through the car park and turn right along the A4361 for 40m. Turn left to cross the road and go through the gate. Keep to the path beside the River Kennet for 1.3km (¾ mile), passing some small gates and stiles; over to the right is the unmistakable outline of **Silbury Hill** (there is no access to the hill).

The 40m (130ft) high **Silbury Hill** is the largest man-made prehistoric mound in Europe, built sometime around 2400BC (late Neolithic), at a similar time to

The unique outline of prehistoric Silbury Hill

the Avebury 'henge' stone circle and West Kennet Avenue. As for why it was built, no one really knows, although local legend attributes the mound to the devil. He was planning to dump a load of earth on nearby Marlborough, but was stopped by the priests at Avebury, while in another version it is a cobbler who thwarts the devil.

Go through the gate and carefully cross the A4, then turn left for 30m. Turn right through the gate to follow a track southwards, and shortly after crossing the Kennet bear left along a path to a large oak tree. ◄ Here a 400m detour to the right (south) leads to the **West Kennett Long Barrow**.

Some people believe the tree has 'special' powers and have tied ribbons to the branches.

The **West Kennet Long Barrow**, dating from 3600BC, is one of the largest and most impressive Neolithic chambered tombs in Britain. During excavations the partial remains of at least 46 individuals along with pottery, beads and stone implements were found.

From the oak tree follow the fence along the left edge of the field to a stile and continue along the track. Cross the lane and stile to follow the hedge on the right as it curves right to a stile and follow the tree-shaded path to a track junction. Cross slightly left and go up the bridle-way to a cross junction; here the White Horse Trail goes straight on. Turn left towards East Kennett, go through a gate and follow the track between the buildings of Manor Farm and continue past Christ Church to a T-junction. ▶

Go right and just before the house on the left turn left along a narrow path before turning left at the next lane. Keep straight on at the junction (the road to the right heads to West Overton and The Bell Inn (01672 861663)), and after crossing the River Kennet follow the track as it bears left and then heads northwards to reach the A4; to the left is a gate giving access to The Sanctuary.

The present, Early English-styled church, which was built on the site of an earlier 12th-century church, dates from 1864.

The Sanctuary, which originally consisted of timber posts, dates from 3000BC. Later a stone circle was added around the time that the West Kennet Avenue, a 2.5km (1½ miles) avenue of standing stones connecting The Sanctuary with the Avebury henge, was constructed. As with most prehistoric sites its purpose remains a mystery, although numerous examples of human remains have been found. The site was first recorded in 1648 by John Aubrey and at that time many of the stones were still standing; however, within 100 years the site was destroyed. All that remains today are concrete blocks marking where the wooden posts and sarsen stones that formed the concentric circles were located.

Carefully cross over to the car park at **Overton Hill** – this is the official start of the Ridgeway.

Official start

Head north along the track from **Overton Hill** car park (SU 118 680). From here it is 139km (87 miles) to Ivinghoe Beacon and the end of the Ridgeway; somewhat nearer it is Hackpen Hill (7km/4¼ miles).

On the right at **Overton Hill** are some well-preserved early Bronze Age (about 2000BC) burial mounds or round barrows in an area known to the Saxons as *Seofan Beorgas* (Seven Barrows). Just to the north the Romans built a road connecting *Cunetio* (near Marlborough) to *Verlicio* (near Chippenham).

This was an Anglo-Saxon army route – 'herepath' literally means 'army path'.

After 2.8km (1¾ miles) the Herepath, or Green Street, which is also the Wessex Ridgeway joins from the left on Overton Down (SU 125 708). ◄ From here a short detour leads to **Fyfield Down National Nature Reserve** (1.4km return). Turn right through the gate heading eastwards across the open field, go through gates either side of a gallop to reach a viewpoint just south of Delling Copse.

Map continues on page 34

Here the chalk grassland is littered with the largest collection of **sarsen stones** in Britain. Known locally as 'grey wethers', as from a distance they look like sheep (a 'wether' is a castrated ram), these stones are all that remains of a hard silica sandstone layer that was formed over the underlying chalk during the early Tertiary period, 50 million years ago. Subsequent erosion broke the layer into pieces, creating the sarsens. Used in ancient times for building purposes, today they support communities of rare lichen and moss.

After exploring Fyfield Down head back to the Ridgeway and turn right.

Continue northwards with views to the west, including the Lansdowne Monument.

> The **monument**, on Cherhill Down about 8km away, was built in 1845 by the Third Marquis of Lansdowne and commemorates Sir William Petty (1623–1687), a well-known 17th-century economist, scientist and philosopher. Heed the saying on the perfectly located seat 'stop and rest a while, enjoy the view, and be glad we can'.

After a dogleg the White Horse Trail joins from the right and follows the Ridgeway for 2.5km (1½ miles) over **Hackpen Hill**. ▶

A bridleway at SU 125 729 heads west to **Winterbourne Monkton** (6.1km/3¾ miles return) and The New Inn pub (01672 539240; accommodation), while a byway at SU 123 738 heads

Overton Hill car park beside the early Bronze Age round barrows – the official start of the Ridgeway

The 145km (90-mile) White Horse Trail meanders through Wiltshire, visiting eight white horse hill figures.

north-west to **Winterbourne Bassett** (5.2km/3¼ miles) and The White Horse pub (01793 731257).

Just before the minor road at SU 129 747 a short detour leads to the **White Horse** on Hackpen Hill. To reach it, turn left through the gate and head down past a small copse, with views out to the north-west.

The **hill figure** – known as either the Hackpen Hill White Horse or Broad Hinton White Horse – was cut by Henry Eatwell, Parish Clerk of Broad Hinton and a local publican to commemorate the Coronation of Queen Victoria in 1838.

Looking up to Hackpen Hill white horse from the road to Broad Hinton

Retrace your route and turn left. The Ridgeway crosses the minor road – to the left is Broad Hinton (3.1km/2 miles) and right is Marlborough (8.9km/5½ miles) – and continues through the car park (SU 128 747). Keep ahead past three picturesque circular beech copses.

The White Horse Trail goes left at SU 131 752 and heads for **Broad Hinton** (4.8km/3 miles) where there is the Crown Inn (01793 731302), the Barbury Inn (01793 731510) and the late 12th-century Church of St Peter ad Vincula (St Peter in Chains) – one of only 15 churches in England with this dedication.

Soon after the copses is a gentle rise from which the earthworks of Barbury Castle come into view. A short descent leads to a surfaced track; turn right for 40m and then left through the gate, following the track past the information boards and up through the earthworks of **Barbury Castle**.

Imposing **Barbury Castle** is the first of several Iron Age hill forts that we meet while travelling along the Ridgeway. Standing on a spur of the Downs at 265m, the double ditch and earth ramparts, first occupied some 2500 years ago, offer commanding views. Jump forward to the sixth century and Barbury Castle is thought to have been where the Britons were defeated at the Battle of Beranburgh (*Beran Byrig*) in AD556.

The surrounding landscape has inspired many including local naturalist Richard Jefferies (1848–1887), who lived at Coate, and the poet Alfred Williams (1877–1930), who lived at South Marston, both near Swindon. A memorial stone, with quotations to both men, is located nearby on Burderop Down (SU 158 762) from where there is a great view (go north down the access road for 200m then right through a gate).

It is eternity now. I am in the midst of it. It is about me in the Sunshine
from Richard Jefferies' autobiography The Story of my Heart

Still to find and still to follow, joy in every hill and hollow – company in solitude
Alfred Williams

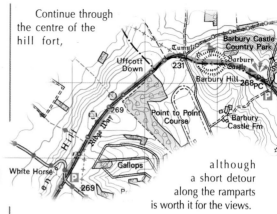

Continue through the centre of the hill fort,

although a short detour along the ramparts is worth it for the views.

The memorial stone to Richard Jefferies and Alfred Williams on Burderop Down looking towards Liddington Castle

To the north, below the Downs, is the former Second World War **Wroughton Airfield**. The six hangars have been home to parts of the science, engineering, transport and agricultural reserve col-

lections of the British Science Museum since the 1970s.

Pass through the eastern side of the earthworks and continue in a south-easterly direction, following the fence and hedge past the toilet block and car park at **Barbury Castle Country Park** (SU 156 760). ▶ Keep

There are plans to develop new facilities here that should include a café, visitor centre, accommodation (including camping) and stabling.

along the hedgelined path to a track at **Upper Herdswick Farm** and go right for 200m.

Turn left through the gate and keep left (straight on) at the split following the broad outline of **Smeathe's Ridge** in a south-easterly direction with lovely views of the Marlborough Downs. On reaching a gateway and cattle grid (SU 175 752) consider resting a while at the seat to admire the view before continuing down alongside the fence to a dip. Go on for a short distance before forking left at the marker, following a path downhill to pass a gateway. Keep straight on towards Ogbourne St George (where there is a pub and accommodation), passing a Ridgeway map, to join a road (SU 192 746).

Ogbourne St George, along with neighbouring Ogbourne St Andrew, has a long history stretching back to Saxon times – the name Ogbourne is derived from the Saxon *Oceburnan* ('Oca's stream'). In the 12th century the manorial rights

35

of Great and Little Ogbourne (now Ogbourne St George and Ogbourne St Andrew) were donated by Maud of Wallingford to the Benedictine Abbey of Bec-Hellouin in Normandy and the monks built a priory near to the present Manor House.

In the reign of Henry V, almost 300 years later, all alien orders were suppressed and in 1422 the estate passed to the Duke of Bedford, and on his death in 1435 the manor passed to the Crown. During the reign of Henry VI the land was granted to King's College in Cambridge, which held the land until 1927. The present church, which stands on the site of the former Saxon church, dates from the 12th century, albeit with extensive Victorian renovations; inside is a brass memorial to Thomas Goddard and his wife, dated 1517.

Alternative finish

To finish the stage in **Ogbourne St George**, either turn right and follow the road into the village, or else cross straight over the road here and head through the trees. Cross a couple of stiles and keep ahead across the field, then go through the churchyard. Go right along the lane and turn left up the main street to the T-junction: to the left is The Inn with the Well (01672 841445).

St George's Parish Church in Ogbourne St George

STAGE 2
Ogbourne St George to Ashbury Folly

Start	Junction of the Ridgeway and a minor road (SU 192 746) near Ogbourne St George, or Ogbourne St George village
Finish	Ashbury Folly on the B4000 (SU 273 843)
Distance	17.3km (10¾ miles); cumulative 31.9km (19¾ miles)
Time	5–6 hours
Height gain	280m
Maps	OS Landranger 173 and 174; OS Explorer 157 and 170; Harvey Ridgeway National Trail Map
Refreshments	Pubs at Marlborough, Ogbourne St George, Aldbourne, Liddington, Bishopstone, Ashbury; shops at Marlborough (and cafés), Aldbourne and Chiseldon; water taps at SU 198 733 and SU 263 835
Public transport	Bus – Ogbourne St George and Chiseldon to Swindon and Marlborough; Liddington and Fox Hill to Swindon, Hungerford and Marlborough; Bishopstone and Ashbury to Swindon and Lambourn
Accommodation	Marlborough, Aldbourne, Chiseldon, Liddington, Bishopstone, Ashbury

Once past Ogbourne St George the Ridgeway begins to climb back up to the crest of the Downs and heads north towards Liddington Castle passing over the highest point on the Ridgeway at 276m; a short detour to the Iron Age earthworks is well worth it for the extensive views. The undulating route then heads north-east along the chalk ridge with the steep scarp slope on the left and crosses over the M4 motorway en route to Ashbury Folly.

Short detours include visits to Liddington and picturesque Bishopstone, where thatched cottages huddle round the duck pond. Just before reaching Ashbury Folly a detour to the south leads to Ashdown House, described as the 'perfect doll's house', while to the north, below the steep scarp slope, is Ashbury, another of the spring-line villages.

From SU 192 746 head south, and as the road bends left towards **Ogbourne St George** go straight on along the track signposted to Liddington Castle (9.7km/6 miles). At the

The byway heading south-south-west leads to Ogbourne St Andrew (1.6km/1 mile) and The Silks on the Downs pub (01672 841229).

junction (SU 194 737) turn left down the track. ◀ Continue along the surfaced lane, crossing the **River Og** and passing through the hamlet of **Southend** with its picturesque thatched cottages. With care, cross over the A346 and take the track opposite past the house (Elm Tree Cottage) where a water tap (SU 198 734) has kindly been provided by the owners.

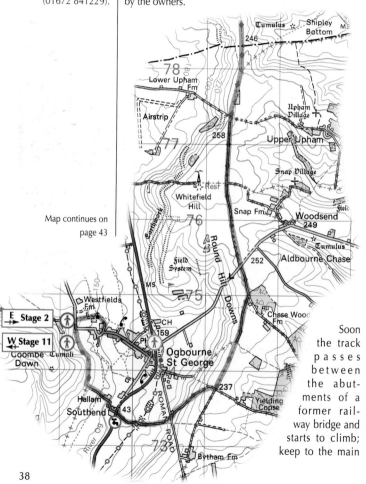

Map continues on page 43

Soon the track passes between the abutments of a former railway bridge and starts to climb; keep to the main

track to join a road beside a house; the road follows the course of a former Roman Road from Cirencester (*Corinium Dobunnorum*) to Winchester (*Venta Belgarum*) via *Cunetio* near Mildenhall, just east of Marlborough.

Picturesque thatched cottages at Southend

CHISELDON AND MARLBOROUGH RAILWAY PATH

The old track bed is now the Chiseldon and Marlborough Railway Path, which forms part of National Cycle Network Route 482. The railway line, known as the Swindon, Marlborough and Andover Railway, opened in 1881 and was later combined with the Swindon and Cheltenham Extension Railway to form the Midland and South Western Junction Railway; the line closed in the 1960s. The path gives easy access southwards to Marlborough with a good range of facilities (5km/3½ miles each way) and north to Chiseldon (6.5km/4 miles each way) where there is the 13th-century Holy Cross Church, village shop, post office and pub – The Patriot Arms (01793 740311, accommodation): the village is also accessible from nearer to Liddington Castle.

The High Street in the centre of market town of Marlborough holds weekly markets on Wednesday and Saturday – the town was granted ▶

its charter by King John in 1204 – and, surrounded by Georgian buildings with a church at each end, is one of the widest high streets in the country. The town is also home to the famous Marlborough College: pupils have included Kate Middleton, William Morris, John Betjeman, Sir Francis Chichester and Chris de Burgh to name but a few. In the grounds is a mound known as 'Maerl's Barrow', on which was sited a Norman motte and bailey castle. Legend has it that the Arthurian wizard Merlin was buried here; however, recent carbon dating suggests the mound was built around 2400BC and is similar, but smaller, to Silbury Hill; the mound is not accessible.

Cross straight over and climb more steeply, keep right to reach a cross track junction beside an old red-brick reservoir. Turn left (north-east) along the hedge-lined track and at the surfaced lane bear left to reach a road on **Round Hill Downs** (SU 214 753); it is 4.9km (3 miles) to Liddington Castle, left heads back to Ogbourne St George and right goes to Aldbourne. ◄ Go straight on, following the track northwards over **Whitefield Hill** (there's a trig point at 261m) – part way along there is a parallel path for walkers in the trees on the left – to a crossing byway with a communication mast to the left; the track to the right leads to Aldbourne (6km/3¾ miles each way) following part of the 19km long Aldbourne Circular Route.

There are other non-road routes to Aldbourne.

Overlooking the village green of **Aldbourne** is the Gothic-styled Church of St Michael, which incorporates many Norman features from an earlier church. Inside there are some fine memorials, including one to Richard Goddard (d. 1492) and his wife Elizabeth of Upham House. There are also two old 18th-century fire pumps, known locally as Adam and Eve.

In 1971 the nearby pub – The Blue Boar (01672 540237) – was renamed The Cloven Hoof for the TV series *Dr Who*, and the village became 'Devil's End'. At one time the village was known for its bell foundries and it was said that there were few places in north Wiltshire that were out of earshot of a bell cast in Aldbourne. At the village pond is The Crown (01672 540214, accommodation) and nearby is the village shop and post office.

The Ridgeway keeps straight on (again there is a section of parallel path for walkers) and soon doglegs right and left; the byway to the west is for **Lower Upham** and the one heading east is for **Upper Upham** and Aldbourne. Ahead in the distance you can see the outline of Liddington Castle; soon the track passes a stand of beech trees with a seat and a great view to the west towards Barbury Castle.

After admiring the views continue northwards. Soon the main track curves right; keep straight on (north) along a narrower path with a fence on the left. Keep ahead through a gate, now with the fence on the right. ▶ Continue up **Liddington Hill**, following the fence and ditch – the route soon passes over the highest point on the Ridgeway at 276m – and keep to the track as it curves across an open field with views to the right to reach a gate. From here you

The path to the left heads down to Chiseldon (3.2km/2 miles each way).

The Ridgeway leaves the main track and heads for Liddington Hill with the earthworks of Liddington Castle visible on the horizon

can visit **Liddington Castle** (1.2km return) for a great view, or continue along the Ridgeway.

Detour to Liddington Castle

To visit the castle turn left, following a permissive path alongside the fence on the right, then go left through a gate. Continue beside the fence on the left before going left through another gate to reach the earthworks.

> The Iron Age fort of **Liddington Castle**, which is constructed of a single rampart and ditch with an entrance on the eastern side, is claimed by some to be the site of the Battle of Mons Badonicus (or Mount Badon) where the Britons, led by Arthur, defeated the Saxons. Take time to wander round the ramparts with their commanding views: north-east to the mast on Fox Hill; just left of this is Whitehorse Hill; south is the mast on Whitefield Hill; south-west is Barbury Castle and north-west is Swindon. The views were much loved by local authors Richard Jefferies and Alfred Williams. The view indicator with plaque beside the trig point was placed here to mark the new Millennium; the quote is from Richard Jefferies: *'haste not, be at rest, this now is eternity…I felt immortality as I felt the beauty of the summer morning'*.

Retrace the route back to the Ridgeway and turn left through the gate.

The Ridgeway continues along the track passing close to a small copse with a derelict concrete bunker. Start heading downhill with the mast on Fox Hill – which the Ridgeway soon passes – straight ahead and the M4 heading off to the right.

> The **bunker** is all that remains of a WWII 'Starfish' bombing decoy site (the name 'Starfish' came from the code name for one such site, which was derived from the original code, SF, for 'Special Fire'). The

site, which was built in 1941 along with one at nearby Badbury, was used to control fires that acted as decoys to enemy planes targeting nearby Swindon.

At the road (B4192; the path opposite is part of the Aldbourne Circular Route and follows a ridge south-east to Aldbourne (6.9km/4¼ miles)), go left down to the crossroads and turn right. ▶

Ahead is Liddington (pub and accommodation) while left heads to Chiseldon.

Detour to Liddington

There's a choice of routes – either follow the B4192 northwards across the M4 and soon fork right down to a T-junction, then right along Bell Lane for The Village Inn (2.8km/1¾ miles return); for a longer alternative (5.2km/3¼ miles return) turn left along the road for Chiseldon (marked as 'Ridge Way' on the map) for 800m, then right at the signpost to follow a path past the buildings and down the long

Map continues on page 46

narrow field; pass under the M4 and continue to reach All Saints Church, cross the B4192 and follow The Street to The Village Inn (01793 790314).

> **Liddington**, known as *Ledentone* in the Domesday Book of 1086, is mostly situated to the north of the B4192, with the exception of All Saints Church, which is located to the south away from the village centre. There has been a church here for almost 1000 years, although the current building dates from the 13th century. The weathered cross in the churchyard is said to be Saxon, while inside there is a Norman font with bead and zig-zag markings.

> Return to the Ridgeway via either option.

Back on the Ridgeway, follow the road (with care), soon crossing over the busy, and noisy, M4 motorway, and then passing the entrance to King Edward's Place (now PGL Liddington) to the crossroads at **Fox Hill**. ◄

The long straight road going NW to SE follows a former Roman Road – the Ermin Way, which ran between Gloucester (*Glevum*) via Cirencester (*Corinium Dobunnorum*) to Silchester (*Calleva Atrebatum*).

Continue straight on and as the road bends to the left bear right at the trees through a parking area (SU 232 814) and follow the track uphill. The Ridgeway now follows a prominent track generally eastwards over the Downs for 40km (25 miles); today's objective is the B4000 at Ashbury Folly (5.2km/3¼ miles). Keep ahead at a crossing bridleway beside a barn and shortly pass just south of **Charlbury Hill** (253m).

Continue along the track, which soon starts to descend to a crossing bridleway (SU 249 823); to the left is a lovely sinuous dry valley, or coombe, that leads down to the picturesque spring-line hamlet of **Bishopstone** (3.2km/2 miles return).

Detour to Bishopstone

Turn left through the gate and head northwards down the valley keeping to right-hand side as the valley widens out and passing a couple of gates. Go through another gate and follow the path ahead, bear left along the road and keep left at the junction down to the village pond; along

the third lane on the right (Cues Lane) is The Royal Oak (01793 790481; accommodation).

Thatched cottages huddle round the village pond in picturesque Bishopstone

Continue beside the pond and turn left along Oxon Place; Church Walk to the right leads to the Church of St Mary the Virgin, which dates from Norman times. There is a fine example of a Norman doorway in the chancel, an old clock mechanism from 1654 and a colourful stained glass memorial window. Follow the track (south-east) alongside the pond and soon go left on a narrow, surfaced path signed for 'The City', passing between some picturesque thatched cottages and a pond. Keep to the path as it curves left to a marker (Ridgeway Circular Route) and turn up to the right. Go right along Nell Hill, soon forking right to retrace the route back up to the Ridgeway and turn left.

The Ridgeway continues on, crossing straight over the road at Ridgeway Farm. ▶ Soon we leave Wiltshire in favour of Oxfordshire and start rising to reach some barns, where there is a water tap on the left (SU 263 835); the road to the left drops down to Idstone. Continue north-eastwards to reach a crossing path at SU 270 841. There are

The road to the left heads down to Bishopstone.

45

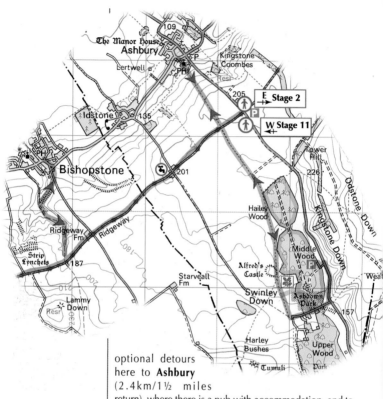

optional detours here to **Ashbury** (2.4km/1½ miles return), where there is a pub with accommodation, and to **Ashdown Park** and House (7.7km/4¾ miles return).

Detour to Ashbury

Turn left through the hedge and follow the path down the field boundary on the right. Go left at the junction and soon bear right past the Parish Church of St Mary The Virgin to reach the main street in **Ashbury**; The Rose and Crown (01793 710222; accommodation) is to the left.

The picturesque village with its thatched cottages, some made of chalk blocks, nestles at the foot of the Downs along the spring-line. In Saxon times **Ashbury** was known as *Aescaesbyries* (the camp of the ash trees), while it is recorded in the Domesday Book as Eissesberie. The church dates from the 12th century, although there have been many alterations over the years. In the chancel is a memorial to Thomas Stock (1749–1803). It was in the church that, as curate in 1777, he started his Sunday School classes for children – which were the UK's first.

Retrace the route back to the Ridgeway.

Detour to Ashdown House

Turn right at SU 270 841, following the grassy strip between the fields to a junction beside **Hailey Wood**. ▶ Go through the gate and continue ahead through the long field, following the fence on the right, with Hailey Wood over to the left. Turn right through a gate and then left, keeping the earthworks of **Alfred's Castle** over to the right.

For a more direct route fork SE along a permissive path to a wide grassy ride and turn right (S) for 1km then left to the car park.

Ashdown House – described as 'the perfect doll's house'

Alfred's Castle is a small Iron Age enclosure consisting of a single ditch and rampart with an entrance in the south-east corner; in the later part of the first century AD a Romano–British farmhouse was built within the enclosure. The fort has been suggested as one of the possible mustering points for King Alfred's army in AD871, before defeating the Danes at the Battle of Ashdown.

Go through the gate and continue alongside the left field boundary; on the way there is a great view of Ashdown House over to the left. Bear left along the track past Ashdown Farm. ◀ Go left at the road to shortly reach the entrance track to the car park and house (01494 755569; www.nationaltrust.org.uk/ashdown-house).

In the field on the left are a number of sarsen stones.

The unusual Dutch-styled **Ashdown House**, described by the architectural historian Nikolaus Pevsner as 'the perfect doll's house', was built by William, 1st Earl of Craven in the 1660s as a house fit for the queen he loved, Queen Elizabeth of Bohemia: unfortunately, Elizabeth died before the house was completed. The house remained in the family until 1956, when it was given to the National Trust, and it is now tenanted.

Retrace the route back to the Ridgeway.

The Ridgeway continues north-eastwards to the B4000 at Ashbury Folly car park (SU 273 843).

STAGE 3

Ashbury Folly to the A338
(Wantage/Court Hill Centre)

Start	Ashbury Folly on the B4000 (SU 273 843)
Finish	The A338 near Court Hill Centre (SU 394 844)
Distance	13.6km (8½ miles); cumulative 45.5km (28¼ miles)
Time	3¾–4½hours
Height gain	200m
Maps	OS Landranger 174; OS Explorer 170; Harvey Ridgeway National Trail Map
Refreshments	Refreshments – Pubs at Ashbury, Uffington, Woolstone, Kingston Lisle, Sparsholt, Childrey, Letcombe Regis and Wantage; shops and cafés at Letcombe Regis and Wantage; café (and water tap) at the Court Hill Centre; water tap near Hill Barn at SU 338 854
Public transport	Bus – Ashbury, Bishopstone and Lambourn to Swindon and Newbury; Letcombe Regis, Childrey, Sparsholt and Kingston Lisle to Faringdon and Wantage; Wantage to Oxford via Didcot
Accommodation	Ashbury, Uffington, Woolstone, Sparsholt, Letcombe Regis, Wantage, Court Hill Centre

This next section of the Ridgeway takes us along the crest of the chalk ridge, passing some truly impressive sites. First up is magical Wayland's Smithy, a Neolithic Long Barrow; then we arrive at Whitehorse Hill, where a short walk past the earthworks of the Iron Age Uffington Castle brings us to the stunning 3000-year-old stylised galloping figure of the Uffington White Horse looking out over The Manger and the Vale of White Horse. It was Thomas Hughes, author of *Tom Brown's Schooldays*, who wrote of Whitehorse Hill as 'a place that you won't ever forget', and it really is a special place. The Ridgeway continues on over Rams Hill to pass Sparsholt Firs and the B4001, reaching the convoluted contours of the Devil's Punchbowl and then the Iron Age earthworks of Segsbury Camp (or Letcombe Castle).

There are plenty of detours to the north of the Ridgeway including Compton Beauchamp, picturesque Woolstone, Britchcombe Farm for a summer weekend cream tea, Kingston Lisle, the famous Blowing Stone, Letcombe Bassett and Letcombe Regis at one time famed for their watercress, with historic Wantage beyond.

WAYLAND'S SMITHY

Wayland's Smithy, a Neolithic long barrow dating from 3700BC, is faced with large sarsen boulders at the southern end. Excavations during 1962–1963 found that it had been built on an existing oval barrow, which held the remains of 14 people in one large chamber. The second barrow, constructed some years later, contained the remains of eight people in two chambers.

The barrow, which is named after Wayland, a magical smith in Norse mythology, was first mentioned in AD955. Wayland was said to own a white horse, and the close proximity of the Uffington White Horse may explain the naming of this barrow. A local legend states that any traveller whose horse required a shoe should leave it with a coin next to the tomb; on returning the horse would be shod and the coin gone. The legend was referred to in Sir Walter Scott's novel *Kenilworth*:

…you must tie your horse to that upright stone that has a ring in't, and then you must whistle three times and lay me down your silver groat on that other flat stone, walk out of the circle, sit down on the west side of that little thicket of bushes, and take heed you look neither to right nor to left for ten minutes, or so long as you shall hear the hammer clink, and whenever it ceases, say your prayers for the space you could tell a hundred – or count over a hundred, which will do as well – and then come into the circle; you will find your money gone and your horse shod.

From the B4000 head north-east towards Whitehorse Hill, which is 3.6km (2¼ miles) away. On the way the d'Arcy Dalton Way joins from the left (SU 279 851) and we soon arrive at **Wayland's Smithy**.

Map continues on page 55

The 106km (66-mile) **d'Arcy Dalton Way** runs north–south between Wormleighton in Warwickshire and Wayland's Smithy, and is named after the late Colonel W P d'Arcy Dalton who worked for over half a century to preserve rights of way in Oxfordshire. It links with four long-distance paths, the Oxford Canal path, the Oxfordshire Way, the Thames Path and the Ridgeway.

Keep ahead at two crossing routes; the first (SU 285 855) gives access to Compton Beauchamp (3.6km/2¼ miles return) and the second (SU 294 859) heads down to the National Trust Whitehorse Hill car park (SU 292 865) and then on to Woolstone (4km/2½ miles return). ▶

Ahead on the skyline are the ramparts of Uffington Castle.

The wall paintings inside the 13th-century St Swithun's Church in **Compton Beauchamp** were mostly painted by Lydia Lawrence, daughter of Sir James Bacon (1798–1895), Vice-Chancellor from 1870 to 1886, who rented Compton Beauchamp House during the 19th century. The present house dates from around 1600, replacing an earlier building that was once the home of the King's Councillor, Sir Thomas Fettiplace.

Picturesque **Woolstone**, home to the 16th-century White Horse Inn (01367 820726; accommodation), is another of the spring-line villages that lie below the steep scarp slope; the stream flows north to join the River Ock. All Saints Church, which is built from chalk, dates from the late 12th century; both the north doorway and the two lancet windows in the nave are Norman.

After a short rise the Ridgeway arrives at **Whitehorse Hill**; the 31.5km (19½-mile) Lambourn Valley Way heads south from here, following the River Lambourn to Newbury, passing through Lambourn (8km/5 miles each way).

Tucked along the Lambourn Valley – known as the Valley of the Race Horse due to the high number of horse training stables – is **Lambourn**, renamed 'Maryland' in Thomas Hardy's novel *Jude the Obscure* (1895). Here there is the beautiful Church of St Michael and All Angels overlooking the Market Place, with a stone market cross dating from the reign of Henry VI, along with shops, pubs and accommodation.

Take a detour through the gate on the left to reach the **trig point** (261m) – the highest point in Oxfordshire – and the earth rampart and ditch of the former Iron Age hill fort of **Uffington Castle**.

UFFINGTON WHITE HORSE AND DRAGON HILL

The stunning Uffington White Horse overlooking the flat-topped Dragon Hill and the Vale of White Horse

The Uffington White Horse is the oldest such horse in the country, and although it was first mentioned in a medieval manuscript from Abingdon Abbey, recent excavations and new dating techniques have shown that the horse was carved some 3000 years ago in the Bronze Age, somewhere between 1400 and 600BC. It was GK Chesterton (1874–1936), in his *Ballad of the White Horse* (1911), who summed up the age of the horse perfectly:

> Before the gods that made the gods,
> had seen their sunrise pass,
> the White Horse of the White Horse Vale,
> was cut out of the grass...

We may know the age of the carving with some degree of accuracy but as to its purpose – we'll most likely never really know.

The figure's remarkable state of preservation has been put down to the 'scouring fairs' that used to be held every several years where local people would gather to help clean it. Thomas Hughes, who spent his childhood in the village of Uffington, wrote about the area in *Tom Brown's Schooldays* (1856), and also about the scouring rituals in *The Scouring of the White Horse* (1859). The small museum in Uffington (01367 820259, www. museum.uffington.net), Hughes' birthplace, is worth a visit for those ▶

53

interested in his life and work (accessible from Britchcombe Farm); there's also a pub with accommodation – The Fox and Hounds (01367 820680) – and a 12th-century church, St Mary's, often called the 'Cathedral of the Vale'. The small, flat-topped, mound of Dragon Hill is where St George is reputed to have killed the dragon. The bare patch of ground is said to have been caused by the dragon's blood, poisoning the soil forever. The steep-sided coombe, or dry valley, to the left (west) of Dragon Hill is known as The Manger, and legend has it that the White Horse goes there to feed.

From here there is a **great view**: to the north is the open expanse of the Vale of White Horse; east-north-east are the Chiltern Hills way in the distance – on a clear day, and with binoculars, you can just see the Stokenchurch transmitter 45km away beyond the power station; south-east are the rolling contours of the Lambourn Downs; south-west is Liddington Castle, with Barbury Castle further on and slightly to the right (look for the stands of trees). A short distance to the north-east is the famous Uffington White Horse – although for the best view you have to take to the air – and further downhill is Dragon Hill.

A signed path from Britchcombe Farm heads north through several fields to Uffington (4.8km/3 miles return).

Having admired these impressive sites return to the Ridgeway and turn left; after 750m a footpath to the left (SU 308 864) drops down to **Britchcombe Farm** (900m each way) on the B4057, where there is a campsite and cream teas on summer weekends (01367 820667). ◄ Soon pass over **Rams Hill** and start descending. A path to the left at SU 318 864 gives access to Kingston Lisle (4km/2½ miles return).

At **Kingston Lisle** – north down the footpath, across the B4507 then right at the lane and left at the junction – there is the Church of St John the Baptist (inside are wall paintings depicting the life St John) and The Blowing Stone pub (01367 820288).

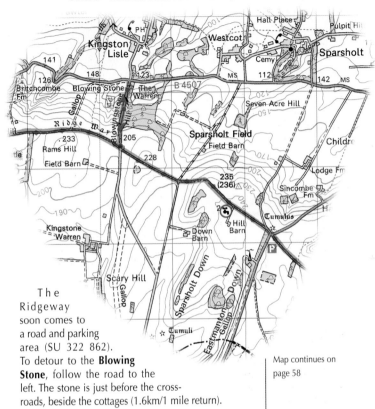

The Ridgeway soon comes to a road and parking area (SU 322 862). To detour to the **Blowing Stone**, follow the road to the left. The stone is just before the cross-roads, beside the cottages (1.6km/1 mile return).

Map continues on page 58

The **Blowing Stone** is riddled with holes and is capable of producing a booming sound, when anyone with the required skill blows into the correct hole. According to legend, the sarsen stone was used by King Alfred to summon his Saxon troops, in readiness for the nearby Battle of Ashdown. The legend may give rise to the village's name, 'King's stone', with the 'Lisle' suffix being a later addition.

The famous Blowing Stone below the Ridgeway

For the Ridgeway, cross straight over at SU 322 862 and head uphill before dropping to a cross track at Collett Bush (SU 330 858). The track to the right goes to **Down Barn** (accommodation); the track to the left heads down to the spring-line village of Sparsholt (5.2km/3¼ miles return; pub with accommodation).

At **Sparsholt** – down the track, right along the B4507 and left towards Wescot, then right at the junction and left at the T-junction – are the 13th-century Holy Cross Church, which houses three rare 14th-century carved oak effigies representing Sir Richard Achard (d.1353) and his two wives, Joanna (d.1336) and Agnes (d.1356); and The Star Inn (01235 751873; accommodation). Sparsholt may also be reached by following the minor road northwards from Sparsholt Firs down to the B4507, going straight over at the crossroads and following the lane downhill, keeping left at the junction.

From SU 330 858, keep straight on up a short but steep rise – just to the right there is a footpath alternative up through the trees and bushes – and continue along the track towards Sparsholt Firs and the radio mast, soon passing a water tap and trough (SU 338 854) on the right just before the farm track to Hill Barn (accommodation). ▸

The water tap was placed here in memory of 14-year-old Peter Wren who 'loved the countryside'.

Keep straight on at the road – to the left is Sparsholt – and cross over the B4001 to a **parking area** (SU 343 851); from here it is 5.6km (3½ miles) to the A338 crossing, to the right is Lambourn (6.5km/4 miles each way) and left is Childrey (3.3km/2 miles each way).

> **Childrey** has a shop, pub – The Hatchet (01235 751213) – a picturesque duck pond surrounded by cottages and the 11th-century St Mary's Church with an unusual Norman font, a one-handed clock and some good brass memorials.

From SU 343 851, follow the wide track, soon passing an old stile on the left (SU 347 846); the path to the left (north) across the field leads to a gate that gives access to the wonderfully convoluted contours of **Crowhole Bottom** and the **Devil's Punchbowl** (this picturesque deep dry

View across the Devil's Punchbowl

valley, or coombe, forms a large expanse of unimproved chalk grassland and is open access land). However, we continue straight on with views out to the left to reach a road at **Gramp's Hill**; the road to the left is one of three access routes down to the picturesque spring-line settlements of Letcombe Bassett and Letcombe Regis (pub, shop/café and accommodation) tucked beneath the downs.

Go straight on, soon passing a track to **Parsonagehill Barn**, then a minor road (second route to the Letcombes) to reach a seat on the left with a view to the north; just beyond is the third option for a detour to the Letcombe Regis, or Wantage, with its range of facilities.

Detour to Wantage via Letcombe Bassett and Letcombe Regis

To detour to Letcombe Bassett and Letcombe Regis then back to the Ridgeway adds 5.7km/3½ miles return; taking in the facilities of Wantage adds a total of 10.5km/6½ miles return.

Go left (north) over the stile (SU 378 841) and steeply downhill, crossing a stile just left of the trees on the way. After a short rise cross a stile, continue along the field edge to a stile and go right down Gramp's Hill Road towards **Letcombe Bassett**.

The lane to the left leads to the 13th-century **St Michael's and All Angels Church**, which retains some fine examples of Norman ornamentation. To the left of the entrance is a blocked-up doorway, and still discernible are the four signs of the Evangelists: the

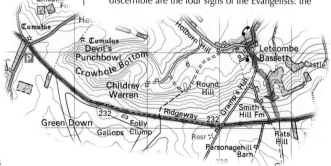

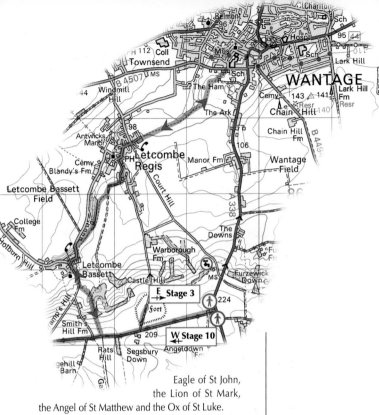

Eagle of St John,
the Lion of St Mark,
the Angel of St Matthew and the Ox of St Luke.

The name Letcombe comes from *Ledecumbe*,
meaning 'the brook (lede) in the valley'; Bassett is
from the Norman baron, Richard Bassett, who lived
in the manor house in the mid-12th century and
'Regis' was added during the reign of Richard II.

Go right at the junction towards Letcombe Regis and
Wantage; the lane to the left passes a thatched cottage
down to the right, which is said to have been the inspira-
tion for Arabella's Cottage in Thomas Hardy's novel *Jude
the Obscure*; Hardy renamed the village Cresscombe. At
the junction with Rectory Lane, take the path on the
right, to the left of the house, signposted for Letcombe

The Iron Age earth rampart and ditch of Segsbury Camp (also known as Letcombe Castle)

On the left is Letcombe Brook, once famed for its watercress.

Regis. ◄ On joining a track (SU 379 860) go left and right to a junction and turn left down the lane (South Street) through **Letcombe Regis** to the crossroads; ahead is the 12th-century St Andrew's Church, left is the village shop and café and right along Main Street towards Wantage is The Greyhound Inn (01235 771093).

To continue to Wantage (adds 4.8km/3 miles return from Letcombe Regis) continue along Main Street to a junction with Court Hill Road and Manor Fields (SU 382 866), from where a signed path heads north-eastwards to **Wantage**.

Cross straight over the B4507 and follow Locks Lane then right along Priory Road and Church Street to the museum with the church on the left; the lane to the left heads to the Market Place.

Famed as the birthplace of Alfred the Great in AD849, **Wantage** offers a full range of facilities. In the Market Place, surrounded by some fine Georgian and Victorian buildings, is a statue of Alfred, King of the West Saxons, who became the overlord of England after defeating the Danes.

Other famous residents have included the poet Sir John Betjeman and the jockey Lester Piggott who was born here in 1935.

The much-restored church of St Peter and St Paul still displays many features from the original 13th-century structure; the restoration was undertaken by well-known Victorian architect George Edmund (GE) Street, who also lived in Wantage. Inside there are some impressive monuments to the Fitzwaryns, who held the Manor of Wantage, including one to Sir Ivo Fitzwaryn (1343–1414), whose daughter Alice married Sir Richard (Dick) Whittington (1358–1423), three times Lord Mayor of London. To learn more about the Vale of White Horse visit the interesting Vale and Downland Museum (01235 771447; www.wantage-museum. com) opposite the church.

Retrace steps through Letcombe Regis and Letcombe Bassett back to the Ridgeway.

The Ridgeway continues eastwards as it drops slightly to reach Segsbury Farm (SU 383 842); the track to the left heads north through the earthworks of a former Iron Age **fort**.

The fort, known as **Segsbury Camp or Letcombe Castle**, consists of a single rampart and ditch structure with an entrance on the east side. Excavations in the 1990s found the remains of Iron Age roundhouses and the 'fort' was most likely used as a domestic enclosure.

We keep ahead to reach the A338 (SU 394 844); a short way to the left (north) is the Court Hill Centre; turn left alongside the A338 for 500m and fork left along the lane to reach the centre (01235 7602530), which has **hostel** accommodation, a campsite, Barn tea room and a water tap, with views of Wantage down on the plain (3.6km/2¼ miles).

STAGE 4

*A338 (Wantage/Court Hill Centre)
to Bury Down*

Start	The A338 near Court Hill Centre (SU 394 844)
Finish	Bury Down car park (SU 479 840)
Distance	9.3km (5¾ miles); cumulative 54.8km (34 miles)
Time	2½–3 hours
Height gain	60m
Maps	OS Landranger 174; OS Explorer 170; Harvey Ridgeway National Trail Map
Refreshments	Pubs at Wantage, Ardington, East Hendred and West Ilsley; cafés at Court Hill Centre (plus water tap), Wantage and Ardington; shops at Wantage, Ardington and East Hendred
Public transport	Bus – Ardington and East Hendred to Didcot and Wantage; West Ilsley to Newbury and Compton
Accommodation	Court Hill Centre, Wantage, Chain Hill, Farnborough, Ardington, East Hendred

The Ridgeway continues marching eastwards along the chalk ridge and this short, fairly level section leads us past the monument to Lord Wantage to arrive at Bury Down. Along the way we catch sight of the Harwell Science and Innovation Campus.

Down below the scarp are the picturesque villages of Ardington, West Hendred and East Hendred, while to the south is Farnborough, where the church has a colourful memorial window to Sir John Betjeman, and West Ilsley.

Map continues
on page 65

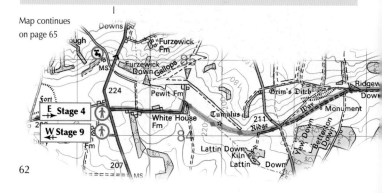

Turn right alongside the A338 for 75m and then left along the track heading east to pass **White House Farm**. Follow the track left and right near Pewit Farm; the restricted byway to the left leads back to The Court Hill Centre (1km/½ mile). On reaching a split beside a tumulus, fork left to reach the B4494 with adjacent parking areas (SU 418 841); it is 6.5km (4 miles) to Bury Down, left heads down to Wantage and right gives access to Farnborough (6km/3¾ miles return) – where there is accommodation but no pub.

The Poet Laureate **Sir John Betjeman** (1906–1984) lived at the Old Rectory in Farnborough for several years, and inside All Saints Church is a colourful stained glass memorial window to him designed by John Piper. To visit the church head south along the B4494 (Chain Hill road) and just after Lockinge Kiln Farm (B&B) fork left, heading south-east on a restricted byway then left at a lane to Farnborough,

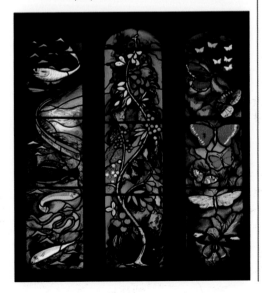

Colourful memorial window dedicated to Sir John Betjeman in All Saints Church

passing the Old Smithy (B&B). At the sharp left bend go right into the churchyard, while for a view of the Old Rectory follow the road for 30m and look left; retrace route back to the Ridgeway.

The Ridgeway continues along the wide grassy track to reach a **monument**.

The monument is to **Colonel Robert Loyd-Lindsay** (1832–1901), later Lord Wantage of Lockinge, a founding member of the British Red Cross and a noted soldier during the Crimean War, who was awarded the Victoria Cross. He was responsible for the statue of King Alfred in Wantage and the building of East Lockinge in the 1860s; he is buried at Ardington church.

Lord Wantage Monument

Head
north-east slightly
downhill to some fir trees and keep
along the wide grassy track, passing a **reservoir**. A crossing bridleway at the trees on the left (SU 442 849) gives access to Ardington (shop/bistro, pub and accommodation), which lies 4km (2½ miles) to the north. ▶

Map continues on page 67

Just through the gate on the left is a sarsen stone and plaque in memory of Lady Penelope Betjeman (1910–1986).

Close to the Boar's Head (01235 833254; accommodation) in **Ardington** is Holy Trinity Church, which has a fine Norman doorway and a 14th-century churchyard cross; inside is a sculpture by Edward Bailey, who also designed Nelson's Column in Trafalgar Square.

The beautifully symmetrical grey and red-brick early Georgian Ardington House, home to the Baring family for several generations, was built in 1720. The Barings – former wool merchants in Exeter – founded the famous Barings Merchant Bank, which hit the world headlines when it was brought down by the unauthorised trading activities of Nick Leeson in the 1990s (01235 833244; www.ardingtonhouse.com).

The Ridgeway continues to pass a trig point on Cuckhamsley Hill (203m); the gate on the right gives access to the unusual earthwork of **Scutchamer Knob** – as for what it was, nobody really knows, although legend has it as the burial site of the Saxon King Cwichelm. Keep

The Harrow at West Ilsley

ahead through the parking area (SU 458 850): the surfaced track to the left (north) heads down to East Hendred (8km/5 miles return).

East Hendred, the larger of the two Hendred villages, has a wealth of 16th- and 17th-century brick and timber-framed houses as well a village shop, three pubs (Eyston Arms – 01235 833320; The Wheatsheaf – 01235 833229; and The Plough Inn – 01235 833213) and accommodation.

The church of St Augustine of Canterbury houses a faceless clock built in 1525 by John Seymour of Wantage, making it one of the oldest clocks in England. Hendred House, also known as the Manor of the Arches, has been the home of the Eyston family for over 560 years. The little 15th-century Chapel of Jesus of Bethlehem (Champs Chapel), built by the Carthusian monks of Sheen in Surrey, is now home to the small, but interesting village museum (01235 835092/821796; www.hendredmuseum.org.uk).

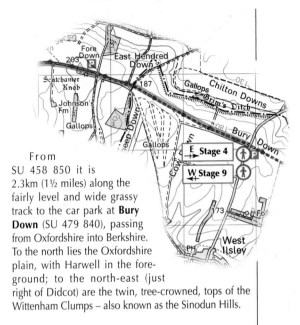

From SU 458 850 it is 2.3km (1½ miles) along the fairly level and wide grassy track to the car park at **Bury Down** (SU 479 840), passing from Oxfordshire into Berkshire. To the north lies the Oxfordshire plain, with Harwell in the foreground; to the north-east (just right of Didcot) are the twin, tree-crowned, tops of the Wittenham Clumps – also known as the Sinodun Hills.

After 400m a crossing bridleway (SU 462 848) gives access to **West Ilsley** (go right across the gallop then bear left alongside the fence for 2.4km (1½ miles) to a road near the Harrow Inn (01635 281260).

Harwell, now the Harwell Science and Innovation Campus, was established in 1946 on the site of a former WWII airfield, as Britain's first Atomic Energy Research Establishment with five research reactors, including the first nuclear reactor in Western Europe (GLEEP – the Graphite Low Energy Experimental Pile), which operated for 43 years. The site is now home to the Rutherford Appleton Laboratory and includes the ISIS neutron source and the Diamond Light Source Synchrotron (the large metal disc-shaped building) – the UK's largest scientific investment for 30 years.

STAGE 5
Bury Down to Streatley

Start	Bury Down car park (SU 479 840)
Finish	Crossroads on the A329 in Streatley (SU 591 807)
Distance	13.2km (8¼ miles); cumulative 68km (42¼ miles)
Time	3½–4½ hours
Height gain	140m
Maps	OS Landranger 174; OS Explorer 170; Harvey Ridgeway National Trail Map
Refreshments	Pubs at West and East Ilsley, Chilton, Compton, Blewbury, Aldworth and Streatley; shop at Compton
Public transport	Bus – Chilton to Oxford via Didcot; East Ilsley and Compton to Newbury; Blewbury to Didcot; Streatley to Reading and Wallingford: trains – Goring
Accommodation	East Ilsley, Compton, Blewbury, Aldworth, Streatley

Shortly after leaving Bury Down we pass under the A34 before heading eastwards towards the Goring Gap; along the way views stretch south-west to the North Hampshire Downs some 25km (15½ miles) away. A final long descent beside Streatley Warren, with views of the Chiltern Hills ahead, through which the eastern half of the Ridgeway will soon pass, leads to Streatley, home to a youth hostel and a pub, with the neighbouring village of Goring just across the River Thames.

Detours include East Ilsley – once famed for its sheep market, historic Blewbury, and Aldworth, home to the 'Aldworth Giants' – nine larger than life effigies of the de la Beche family.

Cross over the minor road that leads to West Ilsley (1.6km/1 mile return) and continue along the wide grassy strip, soon heading through the A34 underpass; the painted murals depict local churches in the Hundred of Compton – unfortunately these are becoming defaced. Go up the rise and keep left to follow the track in a south-easterly direction; a path to the north leads to Chilton (2.4km/1½ miles), home to the 12th-century All Saints Church, as well as accommodation and The Rose and Crown pub

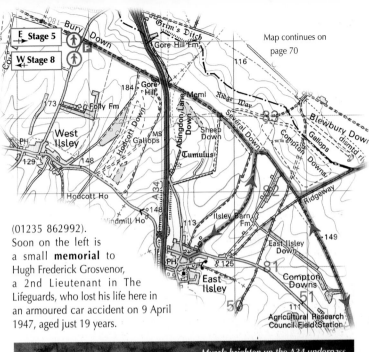

Map continues on page 70

(01235 862992).
Soon on the left is
a small **memorial** to
Hugh Frederick Grosvenor,
a 2nd Lieutenant in The
Lifeguards, who lost his life here in
an armoured car accident on 9 April
1947, aged just 19 years.

Murals brighten up the A34 underpass

Continue over **Several Down**, with horse gallops on both sides and views south towards East Ilsley. Head gently downhill, passing a couple of bridleways on the right; the second one (SU 503 824) gives the easiest access route to East Ilsley (3.6km/2¼ miles return).

Detour to East Ilsley

To reach **East Ilsley**, turn right down the bridleway following the gallop, continue past the buildings and turn right along the road to the duck pond. Fork right for The Crown and Horns (01635 281545) and The Swan (01635 281238), which both offer accommodation.

East Ilsley was once famed for its sheep market, second only to Smithfield Market, London. The market, which started during the reign of Henry III and continued until 1934, reached its peak in the 1880s when 20,000 sheep were changing hands in a single day. To the south (up Church Hill) is St Mary's Church, which dates from the 11th century,

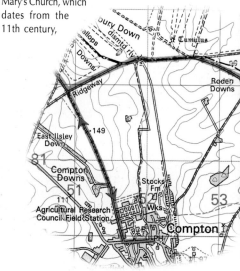

although most of what you can see is from the 13th century.

Retrace steps back to the main route.

The Ridgeway continues south-eastwards, passing the end of a line of trees to arrive at the second crossing track (SU 508 818). ▶

It is 9.2km (5¾ miles) to Streatley, straight on is Compton (4.9km/3 miles return) and right goes to East Ilsley (1.5km/1 mile each way).

Detour to Compton

To detour to **Compton** continue straight on (south-south-east) along the concrete track (later Church Road), then left along the High Street to the village shop and The Compton Swan (01635 579400; accommodation); the village is also accessible by bridleway from SU 518 823.

The Parish Church of St Mary and St Nicholas, which is a short way south-east of the centre of **Compton**, dates from the 13th century. Inside is a Norman font and some interesting monuments including one to Richard Pygott and his wife Alice (about 1500). In between is Compton's former railway station (a private house), which was once an important centre for the transportation of sheep from nearby East Ilsley.

Retrace steps back to the main route.

The trail turns left (north-east) past a Ridgeway map. Follow the track downhill, shortly crossing the old **railway** bridge.

Map continues on page 73

71

The view looking east from Compton Downs

The railway, known as the **Didcot, Newbury and Southampton Railway**, was built in 1881 to connect Didcot and the Great Western mainline with Southampton via Newbury; passenger services were withdrawn in 1962 and the line was finally closed in 1967.

Fork right up a short rise and head towards some pine trees, keeping straight on at two crossing routes. The byway to the north leads to Blewbury (7.2km/4½ miles return – pubs, accommodation and post office); to the right is **Roden Downs**, the site of a Romano–British cemetery.

To reach **Blewbury** follow the byway (SU 534 819) northwards and shortly after passing some buildings fork left down a signed path to reach the A417 opposite The Barley Mow (01235 850296) and South Street; for The Red Lion (01235 850403; accommodation) go left and then right along Nottingham Fee. To visit the church head north along South Street and fork left along Church Road; retrace the route back to the Ridgeway.

Once home to Kenneth Grahame (1859–1932), author of *The Wind in the Willows*, **Blewbury** has many timbered buildings and thatched roofs as well as some original thatched cob boundary walls. Inside the Church of St Michael the Archangel, which was rebuilt in the 11th century and described by Sir John Betjeman as 'one of the most attractive medieval buildings in Oxfordshire', are some interesting memorial brasses, including one to Dame Alice Daunce (d.1523) and her husband Sir John, Surveyor-General to Henry VIII.

The Ridgeway passes another crossing byway – an 800m detour to the left is Lowbury Hill (186m), site of a Roman temple, from where the track continues down to Aston Tirrold and Aston Upthorpe (4km/2½ miles) – and fork left (right goes to Aldworth). Head uphill, soon passing **Warren Farm** and keep left at the split (SU 549 812); the right fork leads past **Streatley Warren** to Aldworth.

Detour to Aldworth
Either take the right (south-east) fork at the junction (SU 540 814) past **Starveall** to The Bell Inn (01635 578272), or fork right at SU 549 812 along the top of **Streatley Warren**, offering a great view towards the

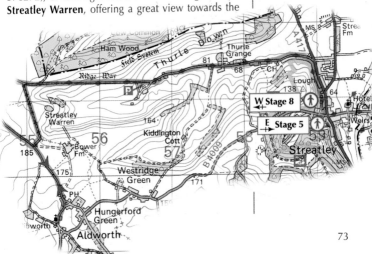

ST MARY'S CHURCH, ALDWORTH

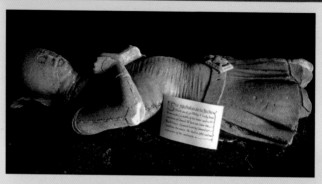

Statue of Sir Nicholas de la Beche, St Mary's Church, Aldworth

Inside the church are the 'Aldworth Giants', nine larger than life effigies of the de la Beche family dating from the first half of the 14th century. The influential family, many of whom were warders to the Tower of London and Sheriffs of Oxfordshire and Berkshire, had come to England in the wake of William the Conqueror and built the long since vanished 'castle' of de la Beche nearby. According to legend four of the giants were known by other names; the largest was John Long, and the three others were John Strong, John Never Afraid and John Ever Afraid. The latter, which has disappeared, is said to have promised his soul to the devil, whether he was buried inside or outside the church. However at his death he tricked the Devil, by being buried in the wall, neither in nor out of the church. The arch where the statue lay is on the outside of the south wall. Although the effigies have suffered some damage over the centuries, they are still an impressive site and constitute the largest number of medieval memorials to a single family in a parish church.

In the churchyard lie the ashes of the poet Laurence Binyon (1869–1943), who wrote the immortal lines:

> They shall grow not old, as we that are left grow old:
> Age shall not weary them, nor the years condemn.
> At the going down of the sun and in the morning,
> We will remember them.

Chilterns, and follow the track to the right, then left along the lane. To visit St Mary's Church, turn right beside the old canopied well – one of the deepest in England at 111m – and follow the lane southwards for 250m.

To return, head north-west from the Bell Inn back along Ambury Road for 800m. Turn right on a track then left (with Streatley Warren on the right) to rejoin the Ridgeway at a junction (SU 549 812), and turn right.

The Ridgeway now makes a long descent, with views of the Chilterns ahead, to reach a small parking area and Ridgeway map (SU 567 812). ▶

It is 3km (slightly over 1¾ miles) to Streatley.

Bear left along the lane (Rectory Road) for 2.4km (1½ miles), passing **Thurle Grange**, and go right along the **A417**. Cross the A329 and turn right to a crossroads in **Streatley**, beside The Bull at Streatley (01491 872392; accommodation) and turn left. ▶ We are now nearing the halfway point, having travelled 68km (42¼ miles)

The youth hostel is 100m further south along the A329.

Looking west over Streatley Warren

The Bull at Streatley

from Overton Hill, with 70.8km (44½ miles) still to walk before Ivinghoe Beacon.

Streatley has a history dating from Anglo-Saxon times and probably a lot earlier than that, although we do know that following the Norman Conquest, Geoffrey de Mandeville was Lord of the Manor. Streatley House in the High Street, built in 1765, was once the home of the Morrell family, former brewers in Oxford; The Bull was where Jerome K Jerome's *Three Men in a Boat* had lunch. Nearby is the Parish Church of St Mary, which dates from the 13th century, although it was largely rebuilt in 1864; inside are some interesting 15th- to 17th-century brasses.

STAGE 6
Streatley to Mongewell Park

Start	Crossroads on the A329 in Streatley (SU 591 807)
Finish	The A4130 just north of Mongewell Park (SU 610 881)
Distance	9.5km (6 miles); cumulative 77.5km (48¼ miles)
Time	2½–3 hours
Height gain	50m
Maps	OS Landranger 174 and 175; OS Explorer 170 or 171; Harvey Ridgeway National Trail Map
Refreshments	Pubs in Streatley, Goring, South Stoke, Wallingford, Crowmarsh Gifford and Cholsey; shops and cafés in Goring, Wallingford and Cholsey
Public transport	Bus – Goring to Reading; B4009 at South Stoke and North Stoke to Goring, Wallingford and Cholsey; Wallingford to Oxford and Reading: trains – Goring and Cholsey
Accommodation	Streatley, Goring, South Stoke, North Stoke, Wallingford and Crowmarsh Gifford

The middle section of the Ridgeway from Goring – where we briefly meet up with the Thames Path – to Mongewell Park, sees us leave behind the undulating contours of the Downs in favour of the fairly flat terrain close to the River Thames – England's longest river. The route heads northwards through South Stoke, home to a picturesque brick and flint pub, before following the peaceful riverside to North Stoke, where the church has some fascinating 14th-century wall paintings; and then on to Mongewell. On the way the Ridgeway passes under the twin multi-arched viaducts built to carry Isambard Kingdom Brunel's famous Great Western Railway, with the Thames Path National Trail on the opposite bank.

Before starting out, a short detour exploring Goring should not be missed, while a longer detour at Mongewell Park leads to the historic riverside town of Wallingford – another good place for an overnight stop.

Head east down the High Street (B4009) in Streatley. Shortly after passing Streatley House (right) the lane on the left leads to the Parish Church of St Mary: this is also the route of the Thames Path National Trail. Pass

The Swan Hotel and Magdalen College Barge on the River Thames at Streatley

the Swan Hotel – moored alongside is the Magdalen College Barge built in 1927 – and cross the River Thames; both the Thames Path and the Ridgeway cross the river here.

The **River Thames** rises at Thames Head near Kemble in Gloucestershire and flows through southern England for 346km (215 miles), joining the North Sea at the Thames Estuary, making it the longest river entirely in England and the second longest in the UK. The 294km (184-mile) Thames Path National Trail follows the river from its source to the Thames Barrier at Greenwich.

We now leave Berkshire in favour of the Oxfordshire village of **Goring**, which offers a range of facilities including accommodation and a rail station. Shortly after passing a café (Pierreponts – 01491 874464) turn left along Thames Road. Anyone cycling or horse riding along the Ridgeway now has to follow the Swan's Way and then the Icknield Way Riders Route by continuing along the High Street and turning left along Cleeve Road – see Cycling and riding the Ridgeway (page 21).

Short detour around Goring

Explore Goring by following this 700m loop: at the café turn right across the road, go down some steps and along the lane, bear left through a gate and continue through St Thomas of Canterbury's churchyard. Leave through the lychgate (derived from *lych* – the Saxon word for corpse) and turn right along Manor Road to pass The John Barleycorn (01491 872509).

GORING

Goring, along with Streatley, is situated in the Goring Gap, where the River Thames flows between the Berkshire Downs and the Chilterns. This has been a major crossing point over the Thames since Celtic times and the ancient Icknield Way crossed here, although the first bridge wasn't built until 1837 – before then people crossed by boat. A few years later saw the opening of Isambard Kingdom Brunel's famous Great Western Railway linking London with Bristol.

The typically Norman church of St Thomas of Canterbury dates from around 1100 and was probably built by Robert d'Oilly, a Norman baron and staunch supporter of William the Conqueror, who held 60 manors including *Garinges* (Goring). The church houses a bell cast in 1290 – believed to be one of the oldest in Britain – while the wooden rood screen (the partition between the chancel and nave, surmounted by the rood – a figure of the crucified Christ, the name derived from the Saxon word for 'cross') is carved out of oak from HMS Thunderer, a bomb-ketch that fought under Nelson at the Battle of Trafalgar. The old watermill and church were painted by Turner in 1805, now in the Tate Gallery, London.

The Miller of Mansfield (one of several pubs in Goring)

Map continues on
page 85

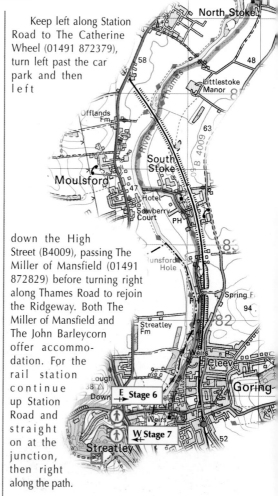

Keep left along Station Road to The Catherine Wheel (01491 872379), turn left past the car park and then left

down the High Street (B4009), passing The Miller of Mansfield (01491 872829) before turning right along Thames Road to rejoin the Ridgeway. Both The Miller of Mansfield and The John Barleycorn offer accommodation. For the rail station continue up Station Road and straight on at the junction, then right along the path.

The Ridgeway heads north along Thames Road, keeping straight on at the junction; as the road bends right go straight on along the enclosed path. Bear left down Cleeve Road and where it bends right into Mill Road go straight on along the right-hand surfaced lane. The Swan's Way now follows the Ridgeway. ▶

Continue northwards, running parallel to, but above, the River Thames, with the railway on the right. Cross the lane that leads down to the Leatherne Bottel riverside restaurant and continue along the bridleway heading for **South Stoke**. Go straight on along The Street, soon passing the 17th-century red-brick and flint Perch and Pike Inn (01491 8724150; accommodation) and St Andrew's Church.

> By the time of the Domesday Book the little village of **South Stoke** had been given to the Bishop of Lincoln and was known as Bishopstoke; however soon after it was transferred to Eynsham Abbey and became known as Stoke Abbas. The abbey owned the village until the dissolution of the monasteries in 1539, and in 1546 Henry VIII gave South Stoke to Christ Church in Oxford; much of the surrounding land is still in their ownership.

The Swan's Way is a 105km (65-mile) bridle route from the River Thames at Goring to Salcey Forest in Northamptonshire, passing through a variety of landscapes along the way.

St Andrew's Church in South Stoke

St Andrew's Church, which dates from the early 13th century, contains some interesting memorials including a 17th-century memorial to Dr Griffiths Higgs (1589–1659), formerly Chaplain to Queen Elizabeth of Bohemia and Dean of Lichfield; he founded an educational charity that continues today.

Go left along Ferry Lane – the Swan's Way goes right – and keep left at the junction to reach the River Thames and a small parking area (SU 593 837), with **Moulsford** on the opposite bank.

Moulsford Viaduct carries the Great Western Railway across the River Thames

At one time a **ferry** operated here, giving access to Moulsford and the Beetle and Wedge; the pub is named after a type of mallet (beetle) used to hammer the wedge for splitting logs before being floated down the river. HG Wells used the pub as a model for the Potwell Inn in his novel *The History of Mr Polly*.

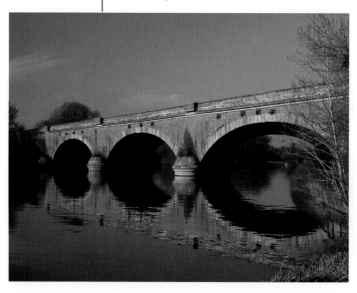

Turn right through the gate and follow the peaceful riverside path: on the opposite bank is the Church of St John the Baptist in Moulsford; later comes a WWII pillbox; and then the route passes under the unusual twin skewed multi-arched brick viaducts built to carry Isambard Kingdom Brunel's Great Western Railway linking London to Bristol across the River Thames; the section from Reading to Steventon opened in 1840.

Just keep alongside the river, later crossing a footbridge beside another WWII pillbox, and soon turn right away from the river towards some buildings then left along the enclosed path to a gate. Follow the path through three fields separated by gates and continue along the enclosed path, passing more gates to enter the churchyard at **North Stoke**, and follow the path past the Church of St Mary the Virgin to the lychgate.

The present church in **North Stoke** was built around 1230 when Robert de Esthall was the

Between South Stoke and North Stoke the Ridgeway follows a peaceful stretch of the River Thames

rector; his memorial slab is located in the chancel floor. The chest is claimed to be a 13th-century crusader chest and Earl Richard of Cornwall, who had links with the church, was in Palestine between 1236 and 1242. The most notable features are the 14th-century wall paintings, which include the Martyrdom of St Stephen and The Last Supper, although some are indistinct and difficult to interpret.

Famous residents have included the concert singer Dame Clara Butt (1872–1936), who is buried in the churchyard; the actor Michael Caine; and Deep Purple's vocalist Ian Gillan, who had a guitar-shaped swimming pool built in the grounds of his Victorian Tudor-style home, which is now the Springs Hotel on the Wallingford Road.

The stream comes from the springs that gives the nearby Springs Hotel its name.

Go along Church Lane and turn left, soon passing the unusual village hall dated 1911, and then the Mill House. ◄ Keep straight along the tree-lined track past

The Ridgeway from Mongewell Park heading towards the A4130

the **golf course** (part of the Springs Hotel), heading north towards **Mongewell Park**.

> **Mongewell Park**, once the home of Shute Barrington (1734–1826), Bishop of Durham, was rebuilt in 1890 for Alexander Frazer in a William and Mary style. Following its use during both World Wars the park became the home of the Carmel College (a Jewish boarding school) until 1997; previous pupils have included the film director Roland Joffe (*The Killing Fields* and *The Mission*) and Sir Philip Green, one of Britain's wealthiest men; the site is awaiting redevelopment. Agatha Christie, who lived at nearby Winterbrook, is said to have used the park as inspiration for the mansion in *The Mousetrap* – the world's longest-running play.

Keep ahead at the junction with Judge's Ride and soon pass between a small lake and houses to reach another junction; here a short (200m) detour left (south-east) goes to St John's Church: go along the surfaced track (yellow arrows), forking right at the split, and then go left through a gate just before some private buildings.

> The partially ruined **church** consists of a small chancel of

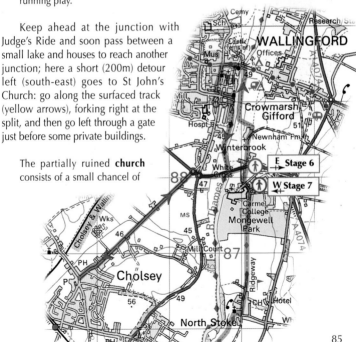

85

Wallingford's historic multi-arched bridge over the River Thames and the open work tower of St Peter's Church

Norman origin with ruined nave walls and a slender west brick tower dating from Shute Barrington's picturesque Gothic restoration in the late 18th century. Inside are two early 18th-century monuments, including one with an effigy of 'a man of sensibility' dressed in Eastern costume and a turban.

Go straight on along the enclosed bridleway towards the A4130 and, just before the underpass, turn right, keeping the road to the left; anyone wishing to visit Wallingford (3.6km/2¼ miles loop), or head for Cholsey, (2.8km/1¾ miles), can do so from here.

Detours to Cholsey and Wallingford

For **Cholsey**, go through the underpass and after 20m turn left then head west along the A4130. Turn left at the second roundabout and continue past The Red Lion (01491 651295) to a mini-roundabout, go right for St Mary's Church (where Agatha Christie is buried), or left then right for the rail station.

WALLINGFORD

The historic market town of Wallingford has a range of facilities on offer including a weekly Friday market granted by Henry II in 1155, making it a good place for an overnight stop. It wasn't until Alfred the Great made it one of his fortified towns or burhs, that Wallingford became important; the extensive earth banks and ditches are still clearly visible. Following the Norman Conquest, a castle was built that came to dominate the town's history for the next 600 years before being destroyed by Oliver Cromwell at the end of the Civil War; in which Wallingford had been a Royalist stronghold.

Jump forward to 1866 and the railway arrived with a branch line from Cholsey, known locally as 'The Bunk'. Following closure in the 1960s the line was saved by the Cholsey and Wallingford Railway Preservation Society, which now operates some steam hauled trains (01491 835067; www.cholsey-wallingford-railway.com). Winterbrook just to the south was home to the world-famous crime writer, Agatha Christie (1890–1976), who lived for over 40 years at Winterbrook House (SU 605 884 – blue plaque); she is buried at nearby St Mary's Church in Cholsey.

For **Wallingford**, follow the bridleway north under the A4130 towards **Newnham Farm** – on the way passing the little Church of St Mary, which has a Norman doorway and chancel arch; the church is in the care of the Churches Conservation Trust (key available locally). At the farm, go left over a stile and continue northwards through the farmyard (barns to the left and a house to the right). Follow the fence and soon turn left across the field then right alongside the River Thames. Pass under the impressive multi-arched bridge and immediately turn right up the steps to the road. To the left (east) is **Crowmarsh Gifford** (pub, shop and accommodation); at 19A The Street (350m from the bridge) there is a blue plaque to Jethro Tull (1674–1741), inventor of the horse-drawn seed drill, which enabled seeds to be sown in neat rows rather than being scattered by hand.

However, we turn right to cross the river – ahead is the unusual open-work spire of St Peter's Church – and continue along the High Street. To visit the church go left into Thames Street.

St Peter's Church is cared for by the Churches Conservation Trust (key available locally). Inside is a beautiful Georgian interior, with coffered ceiling and rounded apse, along with the tomb of Judge Sir William Blackstone (1723–1789).

At the crossroads a short distance along Castle Street is Bear Lane and the colourful Castle Gardens, while straight on is the museum (01491 835065; www.wallingfordmuseum.org.uk). Turn left along St Mary's Street to the Market Place, with its ornate cast iron drinking fountain, 17th-century pillared town hall (tourist information office) and the Parish Church of St Mary-le-More; inside is a striking early 20th-century rood screen, depicting saints associated with the parish.

It was at the **town hall** that Judge Sir William Blackstone presided as Recorder from 1749 till 1770; Blackstone is best known for his law book *Commentaries on the Laws of England* – a book that was also influential in the development of the American legal system.

Follow the road along the east (left) side of the church to St Leonard's Square and turn left along New Road, keeping straight ahead at the crossroads to a T-junction. Go right following the Thames Path towards St Leonard's Church. ◀ As the road bends right, go left, keeping to the Thames Path between houses, and then south alongside the river. Just before the bridge head diagonally right up to the A4130, turn left across the river and soon bear left and then right under the A4130 before turning left along the Ridgeway.

This is Wallingford's oldest church, with some late Saxon stonework in the walls and Norman features inside.

STAGE 7
Mongewell Park to Watlington

Start	The A4130 just north of Mongewell Park (SU 610 881)
Finish	Junction of Ridgeway and Hill Road, Watlington (SU 698 939)
Distance	15.2km (9½ miles); cumulative 92.7km (57¾ miles)
Time	4½–5½ hours
Height gain	420m
Maps	OS Landranger 175; OS Explorer 171; Harvey Ridgeway National Trail Map
Refreshments	Pubs at Wallingford, Nuffield, Nettlebed, Ewelme and Watlington; shop at Cholsey; shops and cafés at Wallingford, Ewelme and Watlington; water taps at SU 660 871, SU 667 873 and SU 697 939 (when campsite is open)
Public transport	Bus – Wallingford to Oxford and Reading via Goring (trains); The Crown at Nuffield to Henley (trains) and Wallingford; Watlington to Oxford, Didcot (trains), Thame and Princes Risborough (trains) via Chinnor; trains – Cholsey
Accommodation	Wallingford, Nuffield, Nettlebed, Ewelme and Watlington

A fairly hilly section sees the Ridgeway meandering through the Chilterns, with the first part following the ancient earthwork of Grim's Ditch eastwards from Mongewell to Nuffield. A short detour here leads to Nuffield Place, former home of William Morris – the man behind Morris Motors. The Ridgeway then heads north, passing Swyncombe and the peaceful St Botolph's Church to reach Watlington. The town, which is a short way north-west of the Ridgeway, is worth a visit, while to the right is Watlington Hill and the White Mark, offering a great view.

A fairly long detour to the west of the Ridgeway leads to the historic village of Ewelme, home to the oldest school in the country, while the nearby churchyard is the resting place of *Three Men in a Boat* author Jerome K Jerome.

Continue parallel with the A4130, but passing through the fence on the right and continue through the trees to a small gate. Cross over the A4074, go through the small gate opposite and up a short rise: the route now follows **Grim's Ditch** for 5km (3 miles).

Grim's Ditch is a well-defined west–east linear ridge stretching from the River Thames to Nuffield (although the name is shared with a number of pre-historic earthworks). The earthwork probably dates from the Iron Age and was most likely built to mark a boundary rather than to be a defensive structure. The word 'Grim' is one of the Anglo-Saxon names for *Woden* (known as Odin by the Norse) – 'the masked one'.

This is a great section of the Ridgeway following a tree-shaded path along the earthwork, soon passing a **trig point (98m)**, before crossing a minor road at **Cart Gap**. Continue across another minor road (SU 636 875 – Ridgeway Map); both the Swan's Way and Chiltern Way cross here, following the lane north–south.

The 214km (133-mile) **Chiltern Way** weaves its way around the Chiltern Area of Outstanding Natural Beauty, visiting four counties: Bedfordshire, Buckinghamshire, Hertfordshire and Oxfordshire.

During late spring and early summer the wood – like many Chilterns woods – is carpeted in bluebells.

Keep straight on alongside the earthwork, soon passing through Oaken Copse. ◄ Follow the undulating path and start rising up through trees to a crossing track with a house to the right; beside the gate is a water tap (SU 660 871).

Just keep straight on, following the tree-shaded earthwork uphill to a T-junction and turn left up towards **Nuffield**, soon following the right side of the

There's a view to the left (north-west) towards the twin tree-crowned Wittenham Clumps.

field. ◄ Turn right

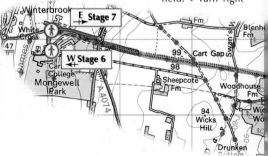

along the lane to the Holy Trinity Church (water tap on church tower – SU 667 873).

Holy Trinity Church dates from the 12th century, with the tower and north aisle being added around the 14th century; the chancel was rebuilt in the mid-19th century. Inside there is a plain Norman or Saxon

Heading past Oaken Copse – a great place to see bluebells in the spring

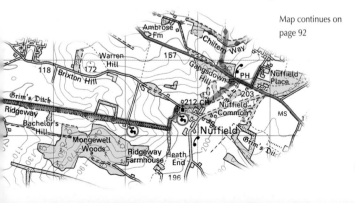

Map continues on page 92

font with a carved inscription and a 14th-century floor brass in memory of Benet English. In the churchyard is buried William Richard Morris, Lord Nuffield (1877–1963), benefactor of Nuffield College, Oxford and founder of Morris Motors – see below.

At the end of the garden on the left turn left and head diagonally right across the fields separated by a gate, aiming for the clubhouse. Bear left across the gravel path and follow the white topped posts across the golf course. ◄ After passing through some trees keep ahead across two fairways separated by a belt of trees and follow the path past a house. Go along the gravel drive and turn left to the A4130. The road to the left heads to Wallingford (7km/4 miles): to the right is the 17th-century Crown at Nuffield (01491 641335) with Nuffield Place a short walk further on; much further is Nettlebed (4km/2 miles), with The White Hart (01491 641245; accommodation) and The Field Kitchen deli-café (01491 641831).

Watch out for flying golf balls.

Detour to Nuffield Place

Map continues on page 95

Cross over the A4130 and turn right (south-east) past the bus stop and then left at the junction to reach **Nuffield Place** on the right (1.2km/¾ mile return).

This was the former home of philanthropist **William Richard Morris, Lord Nuffield**, from 1933 until his death in 1963. Morris, said to be one of the most remarkable men of the 20th century, started his business career repairing bicycles before branching out into motorcycle manufacture and repair, designing the Morris Motor Cycle. This was quickly followed by the first Morris Garage (the initials of which were later used for the MG sports car

brand) and within a few years he started producing cars, the first being the two-seater Morris Oxford 'Bullnose' in 1913, and by 1925 the company was producing 56,000 cars per year; Morris Motors Ltd later became part of BMC and then British Leyland. The 1930s house is now cared for by the National Trust (01491 641224; www.nationaltrust.org.uk/nuffield-place).

From Nuffield the Ridgeway heads across open fields

Retrace your steps to return to the main route.

For the Ridgeway, cross diagonally left to a gate and head north-west down through the trees before continuing northwards through two fields (white marker posts) separated by a belt of trees, crossing the **Chiltern Way** as you go. Bear right at the next junction along a grassy path towards **Ewelme Park** and continue past the weathervane-topped gatehouse.

Ewelme Park was probably established in the late 14th century and was at one time a Royal Deer Park. The present Ewelme Park House is a 20th-century Arts and Crafts building on the site of the original 16th-century Park Lodge.

Keep ahead at the crossing track (bridleway), passing between the farm buildings, and turn right beside a large barn, soon following the field boundary heading north-east then north. At the corner follow the path steeply down through the trees of Jacob's Tent to a gate and continue down beside the fence on the right to a track (SU 678 898).

To the left is the first of two possible detour routes to **Ewelme** (see opposite for the other): follow the track, fork left into the field and go alongside the hedge, then through some trees. Follow the track past Down Farm and at the road go left for 100m then right through a gate heading north-west across Cow Common and continue along the road into Ewelme (8km/5 miles return).

At SU 678 898 turn right up towards **Swyncombe House** and go right at the T-junction, passing St Botolph's Church.

The name **Swyncombe** is derived from the Old English *swin*, meaning 'wild boar', and *cumb*, 'valley'. After 1066 William the Conqueror delegated responsibility for his new kingdom to trusted officers and friends and, according to the Domesday Book, Milo Crispin was entrusted with Wallingford Castle, which included the estate of Swyncombe. The Elizabethan manor house, Swyncombe House, once the home of Alice Chaucer (see below), was extensively rebuilt around 1850. The lovely little St Botolph's Church is of early Norman origin, with a semi-circular apse.

At the junction go left up past The Old Rectory and cross straight over Church Lane to a gate – now also following the Chiltern Way. Head down to a dip, then uphill and continue over the brow of the hill to a marker post (SU 682 913) where the Chiltern Way goes left to Ewelme.

Detour to Ewelme

Turn left (west) at the marker post (SU 682 913) following the Chiltern Way, keep straight on at a path junction and go through a couple of gates. Head steeply down through the trees and continue westwards along the road. At the gentle left bend go straight on uphill still following the Chiltern Way, keep straight on at a track junction and shortly continue along a gravel drive beside a house. Bear right along the road and just after St Mary's Church go left down Burrows Hill (footpath). For the village store and tea room (01491 834467), old watercress beds or the Shepherds Hut (01491 836636) turn right along the road for 200m, 500m or 800m respectively, go left to see the old school and almshouses.

Map continues on page 98

Picturesque **Ewelme** has a church, almshouses and school that were all founded in the 1430s by the Duke and Duchess of Suffolk; the school is believed to be the oldest in the country in continuous use. St Mary's Church has a stunningly detailed effigy of Alice

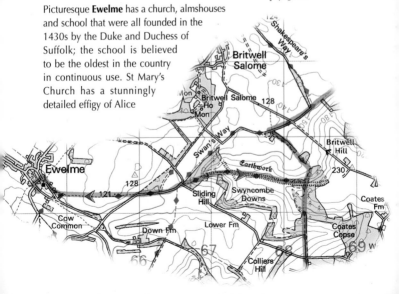

St Mary's Church in historic Ewelme

Chaucer, Duchess of Suffolk (d.1475), as well as the altar tomb of Thomas Chaucer (d.1434), son of the famous Geoffrey Chaucer, and his wife Matilda Burghersh (d.1436), who inherited the Manor of Ewelme from her father.

The manor later passed to the Crown and resulted in the building of a palace by Henry VII, later used by Henry VIII, and the childhood home of Elizabeth I; only parts remain in the present Georgian manor house. The churchyard is also the resting place of *Three Men in a Boat* author Jerome K Jerome (1859–1927).

Retrace the route back to the Ridgeway (7.7km/4¾ miles return).

The Ridgeway continues straight on downhill, later following the edge of a large field with trees to the right; ahead you can see the early 18th-century **Britwell House** built for Sir Edward Simeon. On reaching the old buildings at North Farm, turn right to a T-junction – the **Swan's Way** joins from the left – and then go right along the hedge-lined track to a road and small parking area (SU 681 921); it is now only 1.6km (1 mile) to the B480 near Watlington and to the left is Britwell Salome (1.5km/1 mile). ▶

Cross straight over and continue north-east along the hedge-lined track; after 300m the **Shakespeare's Way** joins from the left for 800m. ▶ After passing Ridge Farm – where the Shakespeare's Way goes right – keep straight on to the B480 (SU 693 932); there is a parallel permissive path on the right – go through the gate and follow the hedge on the left to a stile at the junction with the B480. Cross straight over the B480 and continue along the track with **Icknield House** to the right to reach a junction with Hill Road. **Watlington** with a range of facilities is to the left (2km/1¼ miles return): there is also a water tap at White Mark Farm campsite when open (SU 697 939, 100m to the left) and **Watlington Hill** and the **White**

The Swan's Way now follows the Ridgeway as far as Hempton Wainhill, from where cyclists and horse riders can then follow the Icknield Way Riders Route.

This 235km (146-mile) long-distance path runs between Stratford-upon-Avon – Shakespeare's birthplace – and Shakespeare's Globe Theatre in London.

Take a short detour up to the White Mark above Watlington for a great view to the north-west

Mark are up to the right (800m loop); to visit the White Mark turn right up Hill Road for several metres and fork right up through the trees, keep to the main path (south-east) passing through a gate before heading up alongside the White Mark on the north-west side of Watlington Hill; admire the view before retracing your steps.

> The **White Mark**, an 82m long 'obelisk' was cut into the chalk by Edward Horne in 1764 as it is said that he felt the parish church would be more impressive if it appeared to have a spire when viewed from his home.

Detour to Watlington

Turn left along Hill Road, passing White Mark Farm campsite and keep ahead past The Carriers Arms (01491 613470) to reach the High Street; the Fat Fox Inn (01491 612295, accommodation) and The Chequers (01491 612874) are both to the right.

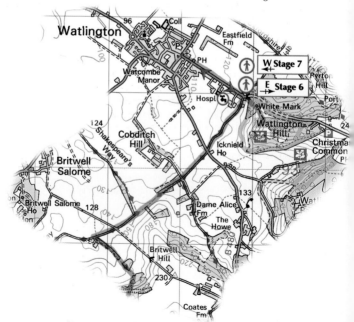

Watlington, reputedly England's smallest town – although it no longer holds a market – offers a range of facilities. In the centre is the Town Hall surrounded by historic buildings: built by Thomas Stonor in 1665, the hall was initially used as a market house, school and meeting place. North-west of the centre is St Leonard's Church, which dates back to the 12th century, although most of the present building is a result of Victorian renovations. Inside is a sculpture of St Leonard – a sixth-century French monk – by local resident Faith Tolkien; he is also portrayed in the west window.

The Carriers Arms in Watlington

STAGE 8
Watlington to Chinnor

Start	Junction of Ridgeway and Hill Road, Watlington (SU 698 939)
Finish	Hill Road just south-east of Chinnor (SP 760 002)
Distance	9.1km (5¾ miles); cumulative 101.8km (63½ miles)
Time	2½–3 hours
Height gain	130m
Maps	OS Landranger 175 and 165; OS Explorer 171; Harvey Ridgeway National Trail Map
Refreshments	Pubs at Watlington, Christmas Common, Lewknor, Aston Rowant, Kingston Blount, Crowell, Chinnor; shops and cafés at Watlington and Chinnor; water taps at SU 697 939 (when the campsite is open) and SU 727 976
Public transport	Bus – Lewknor to London and Oxford (Oxford Tube stops at Junction 6 of the M40); also links to Watlington and Thame; Aston Rowant, Kingston Blount, Crowell to Thame, High Wycombe (trains); Chinnor to Thame, High Wycombe (trains) and Princes Risborough (trains)
Accommodation	Watlington, Lewknor, Aston Rowant, Kingston Blount, Chinnor

Both the Ridgeway and Swan's Way now head north-eastwards below the steep scarp slope of the Chilterns, soon passing under the M40 motorway that slices through the Aston Rowant Nature Reserve to reach the old chalk quarries at Chinnor. The former cement works have long gone, although the large quarry to the right of the Ridgeway has now been designated as a Site of Scientific Interest due to the layers of chalk strata that have been exposed. Chinnor itself is home to a preserved steam railway as well as shops, pubs and accommodation.

Detours along the way include Lewknor with its interesting church as well as Aston Rowant, Kingston Blount and Crowell.

Cross straight over and take the track opposite past the small parking area (SU 698 939) to a junction with a surfaced track (SU 703 945) – this is the **Oxfordshire Way**. A right turn here heads for **Christmas Common** (The Fox and Hounds pub: 01491 612599; 4km/2½ miles return).

The 105km (65-mile) **Oxfordshire Way** passes through two areas of outstanding natural beauty (AONBs), the Cotswolds and the Chilterns, as it weaves its way from Bourton-on-the-Water to the River Thames at Henley.

The Ridgeway continues straight on along the tree-shaded track, later with views of Shirburn Hill to the right. The trees are soon left behind

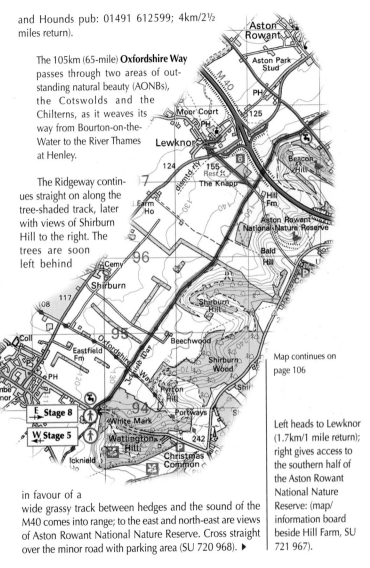

Map continues on page 106

Left heads to Lewknor (1.7km/1 mile return); right gives access to the southern half of the Aston Rowant National Nature Reserve: (map/ information board beside Hill Farm, SU 721 967).

in favour of a wide grassy track between hedges and the sound of the M40 comes into range; to the east and north-east are views of Aston Rowant National Nature Reserve. Cross straight over the minor road with parking area (SU 720 968). ▶

Approaching the M40 underpass with Aston Rowant National Nature Reserve off to the right

Detour to Lewknor

Follow the minor road to the left (NW), cross the B4009 – the former railway between Watlington and Princes Risborough used to go along here – and go left for 40m, then sharp right down some steps and along Hill Road to a junction with the 16th-century Ye Olde Leathern Bottel pub opposite (01844 351482). 150m to the right is St Margaret's Church.

Call in to **St Margaret's Church** to see the carved cylindrical early 12th-century font and some impressive memorials including two large tombs with recumbent figures in the chancel: the one with two children kneeling beneath commemorates William Deane of Nethercote (d.1621) and his wife Isobel (d.1624); the other is the tomb of Mrs Deane's sister, Lady Dorothy Fleetwood (d.1629), and her husband Sir Thomas Fleetwood of Missenden (d.1625). In the Jodrell (or North) Chapel are several memorials, including one to Richard Paul Jodrell (d.1831) with beautifully carved angels by the Florentine sculptor Pietro Bazzanti (1825–1895).

Return to the main route at SU 720 968.

The Ridgeway goes through the **M40** underpass and leaves the motorway behind; it is now 4.9km (3 miles) to Chinnor. Shortly on the right is a gate giving access to northern half of the **Aston Rowant National Nature Reserve** – there is an information board and map showing walking routes.

> **Aston Rowant National Nature Reserve**, located on the steep north-west facing scarp of the Chilterns, comprises flower-rich chalk grassland together with beech woodland and juniper scrub. The reserve, which unfortunately was split in two by the busy M40 motorway, is a great place to see the nation-ally rare Chiltern gentian, as well as a wide variety of orchids and many species of butterfly.

Keep ahead to the A40 and cross straight over to con-tinue past the house with views over to the right of the wooded Chiltern scarp. ▶

Just before the road there is a source of drinking water at the building on the right (SU 727 976).

> A crossing bridleway at SU 734 981 gives access to the B4009 and **Aston Rowant** (2.4km/1½ miles return). The oldest parts of the Church of St Peter and St Paul are Norman, although there have been many alterations over the centuries; there is accom-modation but no pub.

The Ridgeway continues north-eastwards to reach a house and minor road with parking area opposite (SU 741 986).

> To the left is **Kingston Blount** where there is accommodation and a pub (The Cherry Tree: 01844 355966; accommodation). The house is the former Kingston Crossing Halt on the Watlington to Princes Risborough line: the line operated from

1872 but the station was only opened in 1906 to try and increase passenger numbers; it closed in 1957.

Cross straight over at SU 741 986 and continue along the wide grassy strip, passing a crossing track at SU 750 992.

The track to the left leads to **Crowell** (1.6km/1 mile return) and The Shepherds Crook pub (01844 351431); Crowell was the birthplace of the religious writer and Quaker, Thomas Ellwood (1639–1713), whose best-known work, *Davideis* (1712), is a five-book sacred poem about the life of David, King of Israel.

Take a detour into the BBOWT Oakley Hill Nature Reserve and you get a view of the old Chinnor chalk quarry

Soon an old chalk quarry appears on the left of the Ridgeway and just after a path on the right there is a gate (SU 753 994) giving access to the Berkshire, Buckinghamshire and Oxfordshire Wildlife Trust (BBOWT) Oakley Hill Nature Reserve.

An area of chalk downland and beech woodland adjoining an old chalk quarry, this **nature reserve** is a great place for butterflies and flowers including the common spotted-orchid, clustered bellflower and Chiltern gentian – the information board and map shows the permissive path that runs along the south-east edge of the quarry.

These old quarries were once part of the Rugby Portland Cement Company, although the site was originally established as the Benton's Cement and Lime Works in 1908. The soft Lower Chalk is ideal for the manufacture of cement and production peaked in the 1990s, with 5600 tonnes of cement being produced each week. The site closed in 1999 and is being redeveloped; all that remains is the listed 1908 beehive kiln and some of the quarries, one of which was used for part of the opening hovercraft sequences in the James Bond movie *Die Another Day* (2002). The quarry to the south of the Ridgeway has now been designated a geological Site of Special Scientific Interest (SSSI) due to its exposure of both the Lower and Middle Chalk strata.

Continue north-eastwards between high fences, with glimpses of partially flooded quarries, with an especially deep one to the right, to reach a road with parking area (SP 760 002); to the left is **Chinnor** (1.6km/1 mile return) offering a range of facilities including a heritage railway – marked on the map as the Icknield Line.

Detour to Chinnor

Turn left (north-west) alongside the road – there is no pavement to start with, however, there is a parallel path along the edge of the playing field on the right. Cross over the railway bridge – the heritage station is to the left – and fork right along Church Lane to St Andrew's Church. For an alternative non-road route, see W–E Stage 9 (page 108).

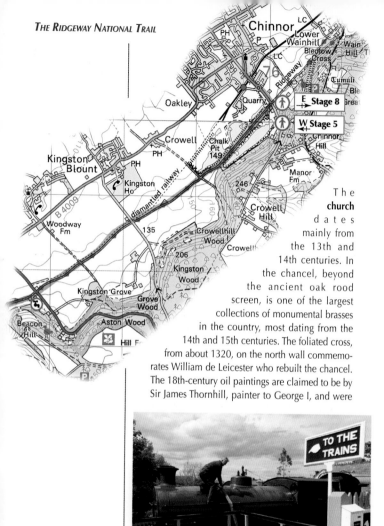

The **church** dates mainly from the 13th and 14th centuries. In the chancel, beyond the ancient oak rood screen, is one of the largest collections of monumental brasses in the country, most dating from the 14th and 15th centuries. The foliated cross, from about 1320, on the north wall commemorates William de Leicester who rebuilt the chancel. The 18th-century oil paintings are claimed to be by Sir James Thornhill, painter to George I, and were

Chinnor and Princes Risborough Railway operates steam trains at various times

St Andrew's Church in Chinnor

used as designs by the glass painter Joshua Price to copy when he was creating the north rose window in Westminster Abbey.

In 1872 the **railway** arrived at Chinnor with the opening of a branch line between Watlington and Princes Risborough. The line closed to passenger traffic in 1957, although the section between Chinnor and Princes Risborough remained open for freight traffic to the cement works until 1989. In 1990 the Chinnor and Princes Risborough Railway Association was formed to operate the line as a heritage railway with both steam and diesel hauled trains (www.chinnorrailway.co.uk); fans of the TV series *Miss Marple* and *Midsomer Murders* may recognise the station. Chinnor's 18th-century windmill, which is currently being restored by volunteers, can be found in Mill Lane (SP 749 010), 200m southwest of where the B4009 and B4445 meet.

STAGE 9
Chinnor to Princes Risborough

Start	Hill Road just south-east of Chinnor (SP 760 002)
Finish	New Road, Princes Risborough (SP 812 031)
Distance	8.7km (5½ miles); cumulative 110.5km (69 miles)
Time	2½–3 hours
Height gain	195m
Maps	OS Landranger 165; OS Explorer 181; Ridgeway National Trail Map
Refreshments	Pubs at Chinnor, Henton, Bledlow, Lacey Green and Princes Risborough; shops and cafés in Chinnor and Princes Risborough
Public transport	Bus – Chinnor and Bledlow to Thame and Princes Risborough (trains); Princes Risborough to Thame via Chinnor and Watlington, High Wycombe and Aylesbury (trains): trains – Saunderton and Princes Risborough
Accommodation	Chinnor, Henton, Loosley Row and Princes Risborough

This short section takes us from Chinnor passing over Lodge Hill with some great views of the Chiltern scarp to the bustling town of Princes Risborough, which offers a full range of services including regular train services. At Hempton Wainhill the Swan's Way, which has been following the Ridgeway since before Watlington, takes its own route, and from now until Ivinghoe Beacon the Ridgeway and the Icknield Way meet on several occasions.

Anyone looking for a short detour should head for Bledlow, used as the setting for some episodes of the TV series *Midsomer Murders* and *Miss Marple*, and home to the Lions of Bledlow pub as well as picturesque houses and a tranquil waterside garden. Or take a detour along the Chiltern Way to visit the historic Lacey Green Windmill.

Head north-eastwards past the parking area and Ridgeway map – a track junction beside a seat at SP 762 005 gives a non-road route to **Chinnor** (turn left at the junction, go through gates either side of the railway, continue along the lane and turn left to reach St Andrew's Church (1.6km/1 mile); retrace steps). Continue past a house

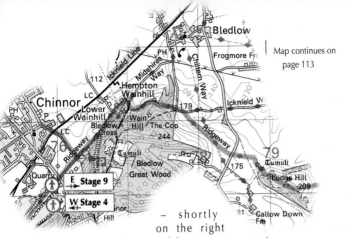

Map continues on page 113

– shortly on the right is a gate giving access to BBOWT's Chinnor Hill Nature Reserve – and head up a slight rise to a junction with a crossing bridleway. ▶

The sunken way up to the right leads to the car park at the top of the nature reserve.

Chinnor Hill Nature Reserve contains a mix of chalk grassland and scrub with plants such as juniper trees, rock rose, pyramidal and twayblade orchid, the reserve is also home to a wide variety of birds, including several species of warbler; the adjacent Chinnor Hill Barrows date from the Bronze Age. A short distance away is the Bledlow Cross on Wain Hill (not accessible): first described in 1827, the cross was most likely cut in the late 1700s, although it is now overgrown with scrub and is on the English Heritage at risk register.

Keep ahead; a bridleway joins from the right (this also leads to Chinnor Hill Nature Reserve and Barrows – 700m), to a junction beside a brick cottage on the right passing from Oxfordshire into Buckinghamshire (SP 770 012); the track ahead – the Swan's Way and **Midshires Way** – leads to Bledlow (2.8km/1¾ miles return).

To visit **Bledlow**, go straight on down the track. Where it bends right, go left on a path across the field to a road beside the unusually named

17th-century Lions of Bledlow pub (01844 343345) – just to the north is the Chinnor and Princes Risborough heritage railway line. (Bledlow may also be reached by following a bridleway south from SP 776 011.)

Head north-east along the main street to visit the Early English-styled Holy Trinity Church, which dates from the 12th and 13th centuries; inside are the remains of some medieval wall paintings and a Norman font. Just beyond is a gate on the left giving access to the tranquil Lyde Gardens situated beside the springs that form the River Lyde (garden open daily). On the opposite side of the road is the Manor House, which dates from the 17th and 18th centuries, and is the home of Lord Carrington, Conservative politician and former Foreign Secretary; the estate has been in the Carrington family since the 1790s.

From SP 770 012 turn right in front of the cottage and follow the track (this is also the **Icknield Way** Riders Route, which cyclists and horse riders need to now follow to reach Pitstone Hill car park) in a generally easterly direction, later rising up to a junction. Continue for 40m and turn right through a gate beside the Ridgeway sign. ◄ Head south-east across the field, soon following the fence on the left (the **Chiltern Way** joins from the left) and just before the field corner go through a gate and turn right. Follow the field edge on the right (the Chiltern Way soon goes right) to a gate in the corner and cross the road diagonally left to a gate; it is 5.6km (3½ miles) to New Road in Princes Risborough.

Walk across two fields separated by a gate and keep ahead at a crossing bridleway to a gate in the far hedge. Turn right following the hedge and keep straight on up the wooded slope of **Lodge Hill**: from the top there are some lovely panoramic views. Go through a gate and past a line of mature beech trees; keep ahead to pass a seat with another great view out over Princes Risborough. Soon go left following the fence steeply downhill; ahead

The Icknield Way Riders Route goes straight on.

Heading towards Lodge Hill

on the ridge in the distance is the windmill at Lacey Green (see below).

Go through two gates and follow the field boundary on the right to the field corner (SP 799 000). ▶ Turn left, staying in the field and follow the field boundary on the right as it soon turns right and passes under a power line. Cross the road and follow the driveway opposite, just before the house (Longwood) take the enclosed path slightly right of the gateway, soon going left through a gate and keep ahead (north) past the **golf course**.

Carefully cross the railway and head through the scrub to a gate (the Chiltern Way joins from the left). Continue straight on up through the field to a gate and cross the Saunderton Tunnel to a junction where the Chiltern Way goes right (SP 801 012); anyone wishing to visit the windmill at Lacey Green can do so from here (4km/2½ miles return).

The path to the south-east heads to Saunderton Lee and then on by road or path to Saunderton railway station.

Detour to Lacey Green Windmill
Turn right and follow the Chiltern Way signs across the field and up towards **Loosley Row**, crossing the A4010

Lacey Green windmill dates back to the 1650s

on the way, go right along Lower Road and then left up Loosley Hill to the crossroads in **Lacey Green**, with The Whip Inn (01844 344060) and **windmill** opposite.

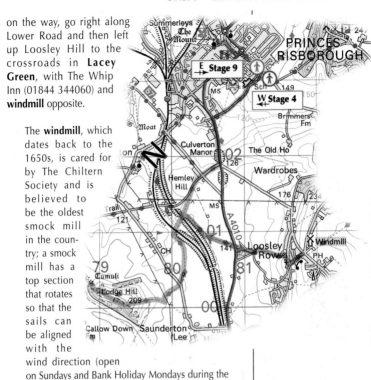

The **windmill**, which dates back to the 1650s, is cared for by The Chiltern Society and is believed to be the oldest smock mill in the country; a smock mill has a top section that rotates so that the sails can be aligned with the wind direction (open on Sundays and Bank Holiday Mondays during the summer; www.laceygreenwindmill.org.uk).

Retrace your steps back to the main route.

The Ridgeway continues straight on (north-north-east) across the large field, passing under the power line. Bear right down the road to a crossroads at Shootacre Corner (the Icknield Way Riders Route goes left along Shootacre Lane) and go straight on along Upper Icknield Way to the **A4010**. Turn left towards **Princes Risborough**, carefully crossing over at the traffic island and use the pavement on the right for 600m to reach the first junction on the right (SP 805 025). ▶

For Princes Risborough Rail Station keep along the A4010, fork left along Poppy Road and left along Station Road.

113

Turn right up along Upper Icknield Way (rejoining the Icknield Way Riders Route), with houses to the left, and follow the track, later crossing a school access road to reach New Road, where there is a helpful map to the surrounding area. Anyone wishing to visit Princes Risborough can do so from here.

Detour to Princes Risborough
This detour adds 1.6km/1 mile return. Turn left down New Road and left at the roundabout following the A4010 (Horns Lane) with the tourist office over to the right.

Notice the **puddingstone**, a naturally occurring conglomerate sedimentary rock composed of rounded flint pebbles cemented together by a more recent matrix of silica quartz, beside the roundabout – one of several in the Chilterns that are thought to have been used as way-markers for prehistoric man.

The Market House in Princes Risborough

Turn right along the High Street at the traffic lights to reach the Market Square and the Market House, which

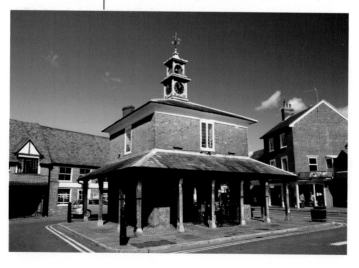

was rebuilt in 1824 as a corn market by John Grubb, who at that time was the owner of the Manor House. Church Street off to the left leads past the picturesque brick and timber 17th-century Corner Cottage to St Mary's Church, which dates mainly from the 13th and 14th centuries; the Perpendicular-styled tower was built in 1907. Next to the church is the 17th-century Manor House, which was given to the National Trust by the Rothschilds in 1925. For the rail station go south-west along Manor Park Avenue then right on the B4444 and left along Station Approach.

17th-century Corner Cottage and St Mary's Church in Princes Risborough

> Known as *Riseburg* in the Domesday Book, the 'princes' part of **Princes Risborough** came after Edward, 'The Black Prince', held a royal manor here in the 14th century; the town has a good range of facilities including accommodation, shops, pubs, bus and rail connections.

STAGE 10
Princes Risborough to Wendover

Start	New Road, Princes Risborough (SP 812 031)
Finish	Clock Tower in Wendover (SP 869 078)
Distance	10km (6¼ miles); cumulative 120.5km (75¼ miles)
Time	3–3¾ hours
Height gain	350m
Maps	OS Landranger 165; OS Explorer 181; Harvey Ridgeway National Trail Map
Refreshments	Pubs at Princes Risborough, Whiteleaf, Askett, Lower Cadsden, Great Kimble, Butlers Cross, Wendover; shops and cafés in Princes Risborough and Wendover; water tap at SP 826 045
Public transport	Bus – Princes Risborough and Great Kimble to High Wycombe (trains) and Aylesbury (trains); Wendover to Aylesbury, Tring and Ivinghoe; Tring to Aylesbury (train) and Luton (train); trains – Princes Risborough, Little Kimble and Wendover
Accommodation	Princes Risborough, Whiteleaf, Askett, Lower Cadsden and Wendover

A more hilly section takes us from Princes Risborough to Wendover, passing three fantastic viewpoints. First up is Brush Hill and then Whiteleaf Hill above the unusual Whiteleaf Cross: both offer views out over Princes Risborough and beyond; after passing Chequers – the country home of the Prime Minister – we reach Coombe Hill, the highest point on the eastern section of the Ridgeway, with a great view out over the Vale of Aylesbury. A final descent down Baccombe Hill leads to the historic market town of Wendover, with its railway station, shops, cafés and pubs, making this a good overnight stop.

A detour gives access to Great Kimble and Little Kimble, where the church houses some lovely 14th-century wall paintings.

The Icknield Way goes straight on.

Go straight over New Road, heading north-east along the track (Upper Icknield Way) and shortly before the end of the recreation ground on the left fork right (east) at the Ridgeway sign. ◄ Follow the field boundary on the right, keep right at the split and follow a path up through the trees of Brush Hill Local Nature Reserve. Continue up the steps, through a gate and straight on up the grassy slope, with Kop Hill road to the right, to arrive at a view indicator and seat.

Here is a **great view**: looking from left (south-west) to right (north) there is the Stokenchurch Mast (10km/6¼ miles), then the twin tops of the Wittenham Clumps, Princes Risborough, Waddesdon Manor and the mast on Quainton Hill 20km (12½ miles) away.

From 1910 until 1925 Kop Hill was used as a hill climb, where the top drivers of their day such as Sir Malcolm Campbell and Archie Frazer-Nash tried to record the fastest time to reach the top; the fastest man up the hill was Freddie Dixon, aka 'Flying Freddie', on his Douglas motorcycle. The hill climb has recently been revived as a historic motor sport event (www.kophillclimb.org.uk).

Map continues on page 122

Turn left alongside the fence and follow the level path northwards through the wood before bearing right. Go up the road for a few metres and turn sharp left; over to the right is Whiteleaf Hill car park (SP 823 035) and information

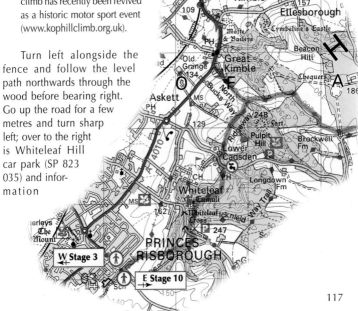

117

boards for both Brush Hill and Whiteleaf Hill Local Nature Reserves. These areas of chalk grassland are home to a range of plants including the yellow flowers of horse-shoe vetch and the blue flowers of the clustered bell-flower, as well as butterflies such as the speckled wood, marbled white and chalk hill blue.

Continue northwards along the stony path, passing a **tumulus**, or Neolithic (3600BC) burial mound, to reach a signpost in the open grassy area.

The **tumulus** is one of the earliest monuments in Buckinghamshire and one of only two Neolithic burial mounds located close to the Ridgeway, the other being Wayland's Smithy.

To the left is another great view, with the **Whiteleaf Cross** below: this chalk hill figure high above Princes Risborough was first mentioned in 1742; however, as for its true age and why it was made, no one really knows; the path to the north – Icknield Way – heads down to Whiteleaf (The Red Lion: 01844 344476; accommodation).

Looking out across Princes Risborough from Whiteleaf Hill above the Whiteleaf Cross

Turn right (east) at the signpost and head down through the Giles Wood, soon becoming quite steep, and keep straight on at a crossing path to shortly go through a gate. Continue down the track towards **Lower Cadsden** and turn left to pass in front of The Plough at Cadsden (01844 343302; accommodation) – there's also a water tap in the garden (SP 826 045).

Bear left down the road for 40m then turn right, following a bridleway alongside the hedge on the left, with a house beyond. ▶ Go through the gate and keep to the wide grassy path up through Grangelands and Pulpit Hill Nature Reserve; the wooded hill diagonally up to the right is **Pulpit Hill**.

It is now 7.2km (4½ miles) to Wendover.

The **Grangelands and Pulpit Hill Nature Reserve** is an area of open access chalk grassland and woodland with a rich array of chalk downland flowers in the summer along with glow worms and butterflies including the marbled white and chalk hill blue.

Crowning the top of the wooded Pulpit Hill (which is accessible by a steep path up through the scrub and trees) are the remains of an Iron Age **hill fort** with a single ditch and bank on the steeper western side and a double system on the less steep north-east and south-east sides.

Go through gates either side of a crossing track and follow the path straight on (north-east), with scrub and trees to the right, before curving left up to a gate. Continue up the steps to a sunken way (SP 829 053). ▶ The bridleway down to the left gives access to **Great Kimble** (1.6km/1 mile return), beyond which is Little Kimble where there is a rail station.

This is the starting point of the 56km (35-mile) North Bucks Way: created in 1972 by the Ramblers Association, the route heads for Wolverton on the outskirts of Milton Keynes.

Detour to Great Kimble

Head north-west down the bridleway to the A4010 and turn right to St Nicholas Church. 900m to the left along Church Lane is The Swan (01844 275288) – The Bernard Arms is currently closed. It was here at a parish meeting in 1635 that John Hampden – known as The Patriot – refused to pay Ship Money (a tax imposed by Charles I without the authority of parliament), and this started off a series of events that ultimately lead to the Civil War.

To reach **Little Kimble** rail station, or visit All Saints Church in Little Kimble, continue northwards alongside the A4010 for 400m and at the junction fork right (Ellesborough Road) for the church, or continue for 300m to the station. Inside All Saints Church is a Norman font, some 13th-century floor tiles, fragments of medieval glass and some wonderful early 14th-century wall paintings, said to be the finest in the county. One of the figures is

14th-century wall painting of St George in All Saints Church, Little Kimble

of Saint George, clothed in chainmail and white surcoat with a red cross.

For the Ridgeway, turn right uphill for a short way and then left through a gate. Follow the path over the open access land of Chequers Knap and start heading down across the slope following a path known as the Cradle Footpath. Turn right at the fence and follow it up a short rise, once through a gate head across the field slightly to the right (east-north-east) to the far corner, with Whorley Wood to the left. Continue along the path with Maple Wood to the right and **Chequers** over to the left, with the monument on Coombe Hill beyond – the Ridgeway will soon be passing this.

> Although there has been a house on the site of **Chequers** since the 12th century, little is known about it. The present imposing mansion was restored and enlarged in the 16th century by Sir William Hawtrey, who guarded a royal prisoner – Lady Jane Grey – at the house for a while.
>
> Jump forward to the 19th century and the house was remodelled in a Gothic Revival style (or Victorian Gothic) for the Russell family. The house was later bought by Lord Lee of Fareham and his wife Ruth, who immediately set about removing the earlier changes to give the house its present appearance. The house was later given to the nation for use as the official country residence of the Prime Minister.

At the corner of the wood turn left through a gate and follow the fence downhill. Go through small gates either side of Victory Drive, which leads left to Chequers. ▶ Continue straight on, passing a stand of trees, to reach a gate and road. Cross over and take the track opposite (also the Icknield Way Riders Route), keeping left of the houses. Soon there is a short section of parallel path: keep straight on at the crossing bridleway.

The avenue of beech trees lining the driveway was planted by Sir Winston Churchill; to the right are the twin gatehouses.

> The 37km (23-mile) **South Bucks Way**, which starts at Coombe Hill (SP 849 067) and heads along the

Misbourne Valley to join the Grand Union Canal at Denham (TQ 053 862), goes to the right along with the Icknield Way Riders Route.

Continue up through Goodmerhill Wood (following both the Ridgeway and South Bucks Way) and once

Following the Ridgeway through Goodmerhill Wood heading for Coombe Hill

122

the path has levelled out go left at the signpost and head in a northerly direction. ▸ When a large barn and field becomes visible to the right dogleg right through a gap in the wooden fence and continue close to the edge of the wood on the right.

The path can be a bit indistinct at times but there are several marker posts.

Turn left down the concrete drive and then right up the road to Lodge Hill Cottage and go left through the trees to a gate and National Trust sign for Coombe Hill. ▸ Turn down to the left and once past the trees go right, keeping the slope down to the left and the trees and scrub to the right to reach the large monument on **Coombe Hill**. Coombe Hill/Low Scrubs car park (SP 851 062) is south-south-east from the monument; to visit **Butlers Cross** (The Russell Arms: 01296 624411) head north-north-east down the steep path then left along the road). ▸

Coombe Hill was donated to the National Trust in 1918 by Lord Lee of Fareham, who also bequeathed Chequers to the nation.

It is now 2.4km (1½ miles) to Wendover.

At 260m, **Coombe Hill** is not quite the highest points in the Chilterns: that accolade goes to Haddington Hill in Wendover Woods, at a height of 267m; it is, however, the highest point on the eastern section of the Ridgeway.

The monument on Coombe Hill commemorates the soldiers who died in the Boer War

The monument, built in 1904, is a memorial to the Buckinghamshire soldiers who died during the Boer War (1899–1902). The handy view indicator allows many features to be identified on a clear day, including, from left (south-west) to right (north-east), nearby Beacon Hill, distant Wittenham Clumps (31km/19¼ miles), Ellesborough Church, Brill Hill (20km/12½ miles west-north-west), Aylesbury Church, Leighton Buzzard and Ivinghoe Beacon (15km/9¼ miles) – the end of the Ridgeway.

This local nature reserve offers a range of habitats including open chalk grassland, scrub and mature beech woods and is noted for its orchids and butterflies.

Turn right (east-north-east) along a broad grassy path between two lines of scrub – do not follow the gravel path. Go through gates either side of a sunken bridleway and continue straight on over **Bacombe Hill**. ◄ Later, fork slightly left to keep to the main path, descending beside a large ditch on the right – ahead are views of Wendover – and continue downhill, later passing a Ridgeway Map and small parking area (SP 863 074).

Heading down Bacombe Hill towards Wendover

Cross over the road and turn right down towards **Wendover**, soon crossing the bridge over the A413 and

railway (on the left is Station Approach leading down to the **railway station**). Continue down past The Shoulder of Mutton (01296 769888) and straight on down the High Street – home to a weekly Thursday market – passing The White Swan (01296 622271) and the Red Lion (01296 622266). Where the road goes left to a roundabout beside the Clock Tower turn right along Heron Path, signposted for the Ridgeway and St Mary's Church.

WENDOVER

The market town of Wendover offers a range of facilities (including accommodation, pubs, shops, tourist information, and bus and train links) and makes a good place for an overnight stop.

The town contains many historic buildings including several old coaching inns such as the Red Lion; at one time it took five hours to reach London by stagecoach. The 19th-century Clock Tower at the foot of the High Street, now home to the tourist information office, was originally built as a market hall and lock-up – the clock tower extension was added later. Just to the north-east along Tring Road (B4009) is a picturesque row of thatched cottages, known as Anne Boleyn's Cottages, ending at The Pack Horse (01296 622075); they (or more likely the land) are reputed to have been a wedding present given to her by Henry VIII. In 1796 the Wendover Arm of the Grand Union Canal was built, connecting Wendover to the main canal at Bulbourne near Star Top End in Hertfordshire. However, due to water leakage the canal closed in 1901. The railway arrived in 1892 and is now served by trains from London Marylebone. Slightly away from the town centre is the Church of St Mary the Virgin: although it was established in the 12th century the present large building is mostly 14th-century, with Victorian restorations. Call in to see an interesting array of carvings including human heads along with fruit, flowers and animals on the capitals of the pillars.

STAGE 11
Wendover to Wigginton

Start	Clock Tower in Wendover (SP 869 078)
Finish	Junction with minor road in Wigginton (SP 934 105)
Distance	10km (6¼ miles); cumulative 130.5km (81½ miles)
Time	3–3½ hours
Height gain	255m
Maps	OS Landranger 165; OS Explorer 181; Harvey Ridgeway National Trail Map
Refreshments	Pubs at Wendover, Tring and Wigginton; shops and cafés at Wendover and Tring
Public transport	Bus – Wendover to Aylesbury (trains), Tring and Ivinghoe; Tring to Aylesbury (trains), Luton and Watford; trains – Wendover
Accommodation	Wendover, Wendover Dean, Chivery, Tring, Wigginton

This short, penultimate section leaves Wendover heading for Wigginton passing through Tring Park and some lovely Chiltern beech woods on the way. While walking through the park you may catch sight of something resembling a small squirrel, which might just be an edible dormouse. Slightly to the north is Tring, home to an annexe of the Natural History Museum, donated by Baron Rothschild.

On the right is Rope Walk Meadow, which has been planted as a wild flower meadow.

Follow the Heron Path southwards towards the church, soon with a stream on the left. ◄ Follow the path right and left to pass Hampden Pond and join a lane opposite the Church of St Mary the Virgin. Turn left and go straight on at the junction beside Wellhead Cottage heading south-east past Wellhead Farm. Continue along the track – Hogtrough Lane – passing **Boswells Farm** and a tree-lined driveway on the right to reach a junction at the wood (SP 881 063), fork left and head up through Barn Wood.

Near the top of the rise the path splits; keep to the left fork, following the fairly level path as it bears round to the left through beech woods and heads for **Hale Wood**. Keep to the level path, ignoring ones to the left and right, to join a road beside Uphill Lodge. Turn up to the right for

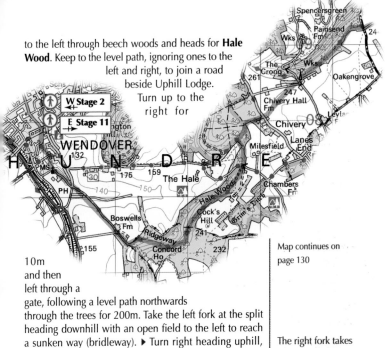

Map continues on page 130

10m and then left through a gate, following a level path northwards through the trees for 200m. Take the left fork at the split heading downhill with an open field to the left to reach a sunken way (bridleway). ▶ Turn right heading uphill, now following the Icknield Way Riders Route again – there is a parallel path just above and to the right – and continue along the track past a house to a minor road (the Icknield Way goes left).

Go through a gate opposite, just left of a house, and head through the field staying close to the hedge on the right to a gate by some fir trees. Go diagonally across the next field, aiming for the **communications mast** and passing a marker post mid-field. Keep left of the farm buildings to a gate and turn left along the road, then right just after the mast to enter Northill Wood. ▶ The route soon splits; keep right, following the level track close to the edge of wood, continue through Pavis Wood and at the far side go through a gate to leave Buckinghamshire and enter Hertfordshire. Keep left along Gadmore Lane towards **Hastoe**; it is 2.8km (1¾ miles) to Wigginton.

The right fork takes a shorter route by heading north for 250m and then bears right to rejoin the Ridgeway.

The Ridgeway and Icknield Way Riders Route now follow each other to Wigginton.

Heading north-east through Hale Wood full of autumn colours

The road to the left is for Tring and the byway to the right (Browns Lane) leads to Cholesbury.

Go straight on at the junction in Hastoe heading down Church Lane. ◀ At the T-junction go left along Marlin Hill for 150m towards Tring (the OS Landranger map is incorrect here – it shows the Ridgeway continuing straight on at the junction along the track; however, signs point you along the road to the left and into Tring Park) and fork right along a track to enter **Tring Park**; there is an information board and map showing walking routes in the park.

Tring Park, which is managed by the Woodland Trust, is an area of broadleaf woodland and open grassland that dates back to Norman times. To the north of the A41, which splits the park in two, is the manor house, known as The Mansion, which was designed by Sir Christopher Wren in 1682. Previous owners have included Sir William Gore, Lord Mayor of London, who bought the house in 1705, and in 1872, Lionel de Rothschild bought the

park as a wedding present for his son, Sir Nathaniel (later Lord) de Rothschild.

The house was taken over by the Arts Educational School in 1945 and is now home to the Tring Park School for the Performing Arts. While walking through the park you may catch sight of the edible dormouse, *Glis glis*: these are much bigger than the native common dormouse, looking more like a small squirrel. Introduced by Lord Rothschild in 1902, the edible dormouse has been slowly spreading out across the Chilterns ever since.

Head northwards through Bishops Wood and then north-east, following the long straight track – known as King Charles Ride – with **Tring** to the north. Later a track at SP 931 104 leads down to an obelisk – known as Nell Gwynne's Monument; the Ridgeway continues straight on.

The portico and ionic columns are all that remain of the former Summer House in Tring Park

129

Detour to Tring

Anyone wishing to visit Tring (3.6km/2¼ miles return) with a range of facilities on offer, can follow a detour from here. Fork left

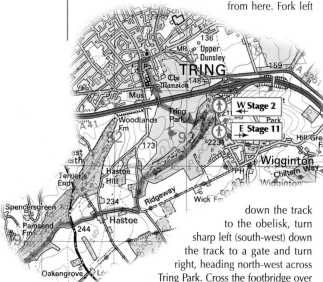

down the track to the obelisk, turn sharp left (south-west) down the track to a gate and turn right, heading north-west across Tring Park. Cross the footbridge over the **A41** and follow the enclosed path before crossing straight over Park Street to follow an enclosed path to the High Street (B4635).

To the right, opposite The Rose and Crown Inn, is the Church of St Peter and St Paul – inside is a family tree for **George Washington**, whose ancestors lived in a house on Frogmore Street – and at the end of the High Street is the market place (weekly Friday market) and the local history museum (01442 827601; www.tringlocalhistorymuseum.org.uk).

However, we turn left to a crossroads and then left along Akeman Street, passing the old Market House, built to commemorate Queen Victoria's Diamond Jubilee (now housing the tourist information office), to reach the

Louisa Cottages

Natural History Museum in Tring, formerly the Walter Rothschild Zoological Museum.

> Opened in 1892, the **museum** originally housed the private collection of the 2nd Baron Rothschild, it was later given to the British Museum and became an annexe of the Natural History Museum (020 7942 6171; www.nhm.ac.uk/tring).

At the T-junction, with the pretty Louisa Cottages – another Rothschild addition – to the right, go left along Park Street and then right to retrace the route back through Tring Park to rejoin the Ridgeway.

On reaching a gate across the track the Ridgeway turns right; the track ahead descends to the white-painted Summer House. ▶ Continue past some houses to Fox Road in **Wigginton**; from here it is 2.8km (1¾ miles) to Tring Station; the Icknield Way goes right to end at Pitstone Hill car park.

All that remains of the early 18th-century Summer House are four ionic columns and a portico.

131

St Bartholomew's Church in Wigginton

St Bartholomew's Church in Wigginton dates back to the early 12th century, with the Weedon Chapel being added in the 15th century by the Weedon's of Pendley Lodge, Tring; the whole building was restored by the Victorians. Much of the fine stained glass was donated by the Valpy family, who at one time owned the Manor of Champneys, about 1.6km (1 mile) south of Wigginton. The manor, which was held at one time by the Archbishop of Canterbury, subsequently passed to the Earl of Norfolk, and later, by marriage, to the Valpy family in 1870. Around 1900 it was sold to Lady Rothschild and in the early 1930s Champneys was established as the country's first Nature Cure Centre.

To visit either the church or pub turn right (south-west) along Fox Road and keep left along Vicarage Road to a crossroads; the church is ahead on left just past the war memorial, whereas The Greyhound Inn (01442 824631; accommodation) is to the right along Chesham Road.

STAGE 12
Wigginton to Ivinghoe Beacon

Start	Junction with minor road in Wigginton (SP 934 105)
Finish	Ivinghoe Beacon (SP 959 168)
Distance	8.3km (5¼ miles); cumulative 138.8km (86¾ miles)
Time	2½–3 hours
Height gain	235m
Maps	OS Landranger 165; OS Explorer 181; Harvey Ridgeway National Trail Map
Refreshments	Pubs at Wigginton, Aldbury, Pitstone and Ivinghoe; café in Ivinghoe and shops at Aldbury and Pitstone
Public transport	Bus – Ivinghoe to Aylesbury (trains), Luton (trains) via Dunstable, and Leighton Buzzard; trains – Tring Station and Cheddington Station
Accommodation	Wigginton, Aldbury, Ivinghoe

The final section leads across one of Britain's great waterways – the Grand Union Canal – and heads through typical Chiltern woods before a final climb beside the deep coombe of Incombe Hole brings us to a broad ridge leading the way to Ivinghoe Beacon. The summit offers a stunning 360° panoramic view – a fitting end to the journey along the Ridgeway. From here you can either head down to Ivinghoe village, with maybe a visit to the Pitstone windmill, or retrace the route back to Tring Station for train services.

On the way a detour leads to the picturesque village of Aldbury, nestling round its duck pond, while further on is the Bridgewater Monument high up on the Chiltern crest, offering another great view.

Cross straight over Fox Road and through the gate opposite to follow the field edge past a **trig point** (216m). ▶ Follow the enclosed path to a gate and turn left along the field edge before going right along the road for a short way to a gate, then left following an enclosed path gently downhill. Cross the footbridge over the A41 and bear right and left down an enclosed path to the **A4521**.

Diagonally to the left (north-north-east) you can see the Ivinghoe Hills and the end of the Ridgeway.

This is known as **Akeman Street**, a former Roman Road that linked *Verulamium* (near St Albans) with *Corinium Dobunnorum* (now Cirencester).

Ahead is Aldbury, with the Bridgewater Monument, built to commemorate the 3rd Duke of Bridgewater, a pioneer of 19th-century canal-building, beyond. ◀

Turn right and cross at the traffic island before continuing alongside the road and bear left through a gate just after the house (Pendley Beeches Lodge). Follow the enclosed route heading north-east with trees to the left. ◀ Turn left along Beggars Lane and right at the junction, crossing the **Grand Union Canal** to reach **Tring Station** beside the former Royal Hotel and Posting Room, which opened in 1838.

Map continues on page 141

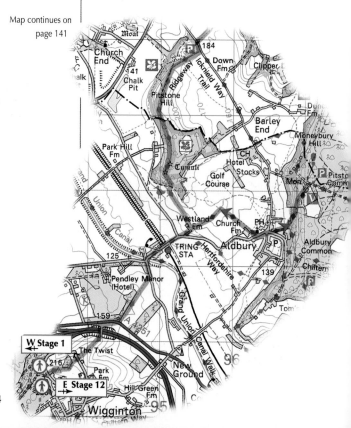

The 217km (135-mile) **Grand Union Canal**, which connects England's two largest cities – London and Birmingham – was formed in 1929 with the joining of several separate canals.

Tring Station is on the West Coast main line from London Euston to Glasgow Central, originally formed from a number of separate lines built by different companies. The section from London to Birmingham, operated by the London and Birmingham Railway, became part of the London and North Western Railway and finally the whole route came under the control of the London, Midland and Scottish Railway in 1923. The first direct train from London to Glasgow took 12½ hours to complete the 642km (399-mile) journey back in the 1850s.

Continue for 100m past the junction with Northfield Road and go left up the concrete track past **Westland Farm** to a junction (SP 954 124) and turn left. ▶

It is now just 5km (3 miles) to Ivinghoe Beacon and the end of the Ridgeway.

Detour to Aldbury and the Bridgewater Monument

Anyone wishing to visit Aldbury (2.4km/1½ miles return), where there are a couple of pubs, a shop and accommodation, can do so by following the Hertfordshire Way straight ahead: this 267km (166-mile) circular route meanders through a variety of Hertfordshire scenery visiting Codicote, St Albans, King's Langley, Cuffley Hertford and Bishop's Stortford. From Aldbury you can also visit the Bridgewater Monument – the loop up to the monument and adjacent café adds 2km (1¼ miles).

Follow the Hertfordshire Way north-east to a junction and turn right to a gate. Keep straight on through another gate and follow the path beside the large barn, go into the field and continue alongside the buildings of **Church Farm** to a gate and keep ahead to the road. Turn left (down) past the Church of St John the Baptist to reach the picturesque village pond complete with old village stocks; just north of the pond is The Greyhound

The picturesque village pond in Aldbury

Inn (01442 851228; accommodation) and south along Trooper Road is the Valiant Trooper (01442 851203).

Pop inside the **church**, parts of which date from the 13th century, to see the magnificent tomb of Sir Robert Whittingham (d.1471) and his wife in the Pendley Chapel behind the stone screen.

To visit the **Bridgewater Monument**, from the pond in Aldbury go east along Toms Hill Road for 50m and take the second track on the left – signposted for the Bridgewater Monument – up to the monument and adjacent café.

The **monument**, part of the Ashridge estate, was built in 1832 to commemorate Francis Egerton, 3rd Duke of Bridgewater (1736–1803) – the 'father of inland navigation'; he built the Bridgewater Canal in 1761 to carry coal from his coal mines at Worsley in Lancashire to Manchester. On a clear

The Bridgewater Monument on the Ashridge Estate offers a great view from the top

day it is worth the effort of climbing the 172 steps for the extensive views (01442 851227; www.nationaltrust.org.uk/ashridge).

Retrace steps back through Aldbury to rejoin the Ridgeway, and turn right.

The Ridgeway continues north-west along the hedge-lined bridleway, soon following a line of mature trees to a cross junction, and go right up past the Aldbury Nowers Nature Reserve information board and National Trust Ashridge Estate sign towards the trees. At the seat bear left up some steps (not sharp left), ignore the next left and head up more steps. Where the old ditch continues straight on keep to the path as it bears slightly left between fences and continue past two information boards, with views to the left.

Aldbury Nowers Nature Reserve, originally known as Duchie's Piece, consists of two areas of chalk grassland joined by the Ridgeway. Cared for by the Hertfordshire and Middlesex Wildlife Trust, the reserve is a great place to see butterflies – the helpful information board gives pictures of many that can be seen along with the most likely dates. Flowers include the common milkwort, common rock rose, clustered bellflower and lady's bedstraw. The reserve is also home to glow worms (the wingless females of a type of beetle), which can be seen during summer evenings when they 'light up' a special segment in their tails to attract a mate.

Go through the gate – now leaving Hertfordshire in favour of Buckinghamshire – and continue straight on following Grim's Ditch (we met a different Grim's Ditch near Nuffield) uphill before leaving the earthwork and heading along the broad ridge of **Pitstone Hill** with views to the left and ahead to Steps Hill and Beacon Hill.

Stand on the summit of Pitstone Hill and take in the **views**: look west back along the Chiltern scarp with the Tring Reservoirs, built to supply water to the Grand Union Canal out on the flat plain with Aylesbury beyond; much nearer is the partly flooded chalk quarry that was once part of the Pitstone cement works, which operated from 1937 to 1991. Just to the right of the quarry is the tower of Pitstone's St Mary's Church; continuing round is Pitstone windmill and then the distinctive spire of St Mary the Virgin's Church in Ivinghoe to the north and Ivinghoe Beacon to the north-east.

Keep to the right at the split (the other path heads up the short rise and then directly to the car park) and follow the fence on the right to a gate at the corner, keep ahead (car park to the left) to the road where the **Icknield Way** Riders Route joins from the right. Turn left and at the entrance to Pitstone Hill **car park** (SP 955 149) turn right through a gate. ▸

The end of the Ridgeway is now close, albeit with a bit of a climb still to go.

Follow the fence on the right and continue straight on past the warning sign (this area was once used for

Heading north over Steps Hill towards Ivinghoe Beacon and the end of the Ridgeway

military training – so **do not touch any unidentified objects**), heading up beside the deep hollow, or coombe, of Incombe Hole. Don't go through the gate but keep alongside the fence on the right and head over **Steps Hill**, looking out for the marker post. Follow the path through the bushes and then alongside the fence down to a gate. Continue along the path and soon drop down to a minor road. ◄

500m to the right – with a parallel path in the trees on the left side – is Ivinghoe Beacon car park (SP 963 159).

Cross straight over (the path to the right is both the Icknield Way and Ridgeway Link walk towards Dunstable) and keep to the middle path, passing just right of the grassy knoll, and continue up along the broad ridge (marker posts) to the trig point (230m) on Ivinghoe Beacon – marked on the map as **Beacon Hill**. ◄

From here, on a clear day, there is a great panoramic view – a fitting end to the journey along the Ridgeway.

Beacon Hill, a favoured location for model plane flyers, was the site of an Iron Age hill fort, although little remains today. To the south-west views stretch

The summit of Ivinghoe Beacon marking the end or start of the Ridgeway with a great panoramic view

back along the Chiltern scarp; moving right are the Tring Reservoirs. Continue across the flat expanse of the Vale of Aylesbury and to the north is Leighton Buzzard, with Milton Keynes beyond; to the north-east is the nearby church at Edlesborough, while to the east are views along the broad ridge past Gallows Hill to the white chalk figure of the Whipsnade Lion on the side of the Dunstable Downs. It took 18 months to make the huge figure, which was completed in 1933.

From Beacon Hill the 13km (8-mile) Two Ridges Link path heads to Leighton Buzzard – starting point of the 64km (40-mile) Greensand Ridge Walk.

Having reached the end of the trail you now have a couple of choices: either head to **Ivinghoe**, where there is a pub, café, accommodation and bus links (adds 2.8km/1¾ miles); or head for a train station.

Route to Ivinghoe village

Retrace the route back to the minor road and turn right for a few metres before forking left down a track. Go left over a stile and follow the fence on the right to another stile. Turn right and head north-west across the field soon following an old fence to join the B489 opposite **Town Farm** (camping) and turn left to a T-junction; to visit **Pitstone Windmill** turn left and at the left bend go right through the small parking area and follow a path south-west across the field to the mill.

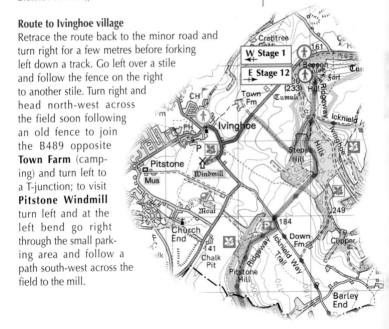

The early 17th-century Pitstone Windmill with the Ivinghoe Hills in the background

Pitstone windmill dates from 1627 and is possibly the oldest post mill in England; post mill means that the complete windmill rotates round on the post to align the sails to the wind (01442 851227; www.nationaltrust.org.uk/pitstone-windmill).

Turn right following the B488 into **Ivinghoe**, passing the Church of St Mary the Virgin – along Vicarage Lane on the right is The Rose and Crown (01296 668472) – to a junction beside the village green and King's Head restaurant.

The cruciform-shaped **Church of St Mary the Virgin**, which dates from the early 13th century, dominates the centre of Ivinghoe. Inside there are some interesting 15th-century bench ends (or poppy-heads), a Jacobean pulpit and large carved wooden angels in the roof. Outside on the churchyard wall is an old man trap and a long pole with a hooked end – used to pull burning straw off thatched houses to

prevent the fire from spreading. Ford End Watermill, first recorded in 1616, is the only working watermill left in Buckinghamshire (01442 825421; www. fordendwatermill.co.uk).

The wonderful lines of the Church of St Mary the Virgin in Ivinghoe

Straight on along the High Street, which leads to Pitstone where there are a couple of pubs and a shop, is a tea room, and to the right 600m along Station Road is Ford End Watermill.

For train services
Follow the Ridgeway back to **Tring Station** (5.7km/3½ miles), or head for Ivinghoe and follow the B488 north-westwards to Cheddington Station (6.5km/4 miles); also accessible by bus.

THE RIDGEWAY
East to West: Ivinghoe Beacon to Overton Hill

The Ridgeway heading towards the town centre in Wendover having passed the Church of St Mary the Virgin (W–E Stage 11; E–W Stage 2)

STAGE 1

Ivinghoe Beacon to Wigginton

Start	Ivinghoe Beacon (SP 959 168), or junction of the B488 and B489 in Ivinghoe (SP 945 161)
Finish	Junction with minor road in Wigginton (SP 934 105)
Distance	8.3km (5¼ miles); cumulative 8.3km (5¼ miles)
Time	2½–3 hours
Height gain	230m
Note	For information on maps and facilities en route see West-to-East Stage 12 (page 133).

The first stage starts out on a high – namely Ivinghoe Beacon, with a stunning 360° panoramic view – then heads south along a broad ridge before dropping down past steep-sided Incombe Hole. It then meanders through typical Chiltern woods before crossing one of Britain's great waterways – the Grand Union Canal – to reach Wigginton. For an alternative start take in a walk from the picturesque village of Ivinghoe before heading up to the official start of the Ridgeway.

On the way a detour leads to the picturesque village of Aldbury nestling round its duck pond, while further on is the Bridgewater Monument high up on the Chiltern crest offering another great view.

Alternative start from Ivinghoe

▶ From the centre of Ivinghoe go along Church Road with the Church of St Mary the Virgin on the right and soon turn left on the B489 towards Dunstable; to visit Pitstone Windmill keep ahead and at the bend go right following a path across the field to the windmill. At Town Farm turn right following a path south-east along the field edge and continue straight on to a stile. Turn left, following the fence on the left to another stile and fork right up through the bushes to a minor road. Go right up to the bend then left up along the broad ridge to the trig point on Ivinghoe Beacon from where the Ridgeway starts, or

See maps from pages 141–134.

Looking south from Ivinghoe Beacon towards Steps Hill at the start of the Ridgeway

To the left is Ivinghoe Beacon car park (SP 963 159).

ends depending on which direction you are walking (this adds 2.8km/1¾ miles).

Official start

From the trig point (230m) on Ivinghoe Beacon – marked as **Beacon Hill** on the map – head south along the broad grassy ridge to a minor road. ◄ Cross straight over (it is 5.2km/3¼ miles to Tring Station) and follow the Ridgeway in a south-south-easterly direction, pass through some scrub and over **Steps Hill**: this area was once used for military training, so **do not touch any unidentified objects**. Head downhill keeping the fence to the left and the deep hollow of Incombe Hole to the right. Continue down the curving track to head south-west and then straight on alongside the fence to a gate and minor road opposite the car park entrance (SP 955 149).

Turn left along the road for a short way and then right through a gap in the hedge passing the end of the car park (the Icknield Way Riders Route continues along the road). Go through the gate and follow the fence before heading along the broad ridge of Pitstone Hill. ▶ Start descending, soon following Grim's Ditch and go through a gate at Aldbury Nowers Nature Reserve, leaving Buckinghamshire in favour of Hertfordshire. Keep to the main path, passing two sections of steps to reach the edge of the trees by a seat. Follow the enclosed path down past the Aldbury Nowers information board and go left at the cross junction following a line of mature trees to another junction. The Hertfordshire Way goes left here, and anyone wishing to visit **Aldbury** should detour left. ▶

Turn right down to the road and bear right to pass **Tring Station** and, after crossing the **Grand Union Canal**, turn left along Beggars Lane for 150m. Turn right at the sign and follow the track south-west, soon with the trees to the right. Pass a couple of gates and turn right alongside the A4521. ▶ Cross over at the traffic island and continue westwards before turning left up a path, soon crossing a bridge over the A41. Head south-west up the enclosed path and turn right along the lane for a few metres, then

Views to the right include both Ivinghoe and Pitstone churches as well as Pitstone windmill.

See page 135.

This was a Roman Road – Akeman Street – linking *Verulamium* (near St Albans) with *Corinium Dobunnorum* (now Cirencester).

The Ridgeway passes some steps at Aldbury Nowers Nature Reserve

The Greyhound at Wigginton

left through a gate and follow the field edge. Go through a gate and along the enclosed path before following the field edge on the left past a **trig point** (216m) to a gate and minor road in **Wigginton**.

STAGE 2

Wigginton to Wendover

Start	Junction with minor road in Wigginton (SP 934 105)
Finish	Clock Tower in Wendover (SP 869 078)
Distance	10km (6¼ miles); cumulative 18.3km (11½ miles)
Time	2¾–3½ hours
Height gain	160m
Note	For information on maps and facilities en route see West-to-East Stage 11 (page 126).

This short second stage leaves Wigginton heading for the historic market town of Wendover, with its railway station, shops, cafés and pubs, making this a good overnight stop.

On the way the route passes through Tring Park and some lovely Chiltern beech woods. While walking through the park you may catch sight of something resembling a small squirrel, which might just be an edible dormouse. Slightly to the north is Tring, home to an annexe of the Natural History Museum, donated by Baron Rothschild.

▶ Cross straight over and follow the gravel track past the houses to enter **Tring Park** (parts of this section also follow the Icknield Way Riders Route). Continue along the track to a junction with a gate on the right (to the right leads to the white-painted Summer House and straight ahead drops down to the obelisk from where a detour to **Tring** can be followed. ▶ Turn left along the track – King Charles Ride – which later curves left to head southwards through Bishop's Wood to a gate. Bear left along the road and then right along Church Lane to a crossroads in **Hastoe**; Tring is to the right and the byway to the left (Browns Lane) heads for Cholesbury. Go straight on along Gadmore Lane and at the left bend keep ahead through the gate, leaving Hertfordshire and entering Buckinghamshire.

See maps from pages 130–127.

See page 130.

The Ridgeway passes through Tring Park – here in full autumn colours

Follow the level track through trees of Pavis Wood and Northill Wood, keeping close to the left edge. Turn left along the minor road, passing a communications mast, and immediately after the driveway on the right go right through a gate with some old farm buildings on the left. Head south-west across the field aiming for the fir trees and passing a marker post mid-field; go through the gate and follow the left-hand field boundary to a gate in the corner.

Cross straight over the minor road (it is now 5.2km/3¼ miles to Wendover) and follow the track opposite with a house to the left, ignore a path to the left and start to descend the sunken way (bridleway). At the sign turn left uphill with an open field to the right, continue along the level path southwards through the wood to a gate and minor road. Go right and then left at Uphill Lodge, heading south-west through **Hale Wood** for 1.6km (1 mile); ignore paths to the right and left. Follow the bridleway as it curves right and descends through Barn

Wood; at the junction (SP 881 063) go right along the track – Hogtrough Lane – to pass **Boswells Farm** and then Wellhead Farm to a junction beside Wellhead Cottage.

Go straight on (north-west) along the lane to the Church of St Mary the Virgin and turn right onto a path past Hampden Pond. Bear right and left to follow a stream on the right and keep ahead to the High Street in **Wendover**, with the Clock Tower to the right.

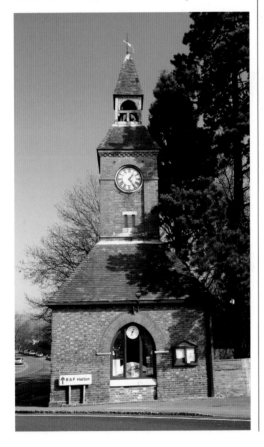

The 19th-century Clock Tower in Wendover

STAGE 3
Wendover to Princes Risborough

Start	Clock Tower in Wendover (SP 869 078)
Finish	New Road, Princes Risborough (SP 812 031)
Distance	10km (6¼ miles); cumulative 28.3km (17¾ miles)
Time	3–3¾ hours
Height gain	365m
Note	For information on maps and facilities en route see West-to-East Stage 10 (page 116).

A more hilly section takes us from Wendover to Princes Risborough, passing three fantastic viewpoints. After an initial climb out of Wendover we reach the first of these viewpoints – Coombe Hill, the highest point on the eastern section of the Ridgeway with a great view out over the Vale of Aylesbury. After passing Chequers – the country home of the Prime Minister – we arrive at Whiteleaf Hill above the unusual Whiteleaf Cross and then Brush Hill, both offering views out over Princes Risborough and beyond. The bustling town of Princes Risborough offers a full range of services including regular train services. For description of a detour there, see page 114.

A detour gives access to both Great Kimble and Little Kimble, where the church houses some lovely 14th-century wall paintings.

See maps from pages 122–117.

◄ Turn left (south-west) up the High Street and Pound Street (the **rail station** is along Station Approach on the right), cross the bridge over the railway and A413 and continue past some houses. As the road bends right go left across the road and along the track (Ridgeway Map – SP 863 074), keeping right at the first split, then left at the next to enter Bacombe Hill Local Nature Reserve.

To the south is the Coombe Hill/Low Scrubs car park (SP 851 062); the path to the north drops down to Butlers Cross.

Head up **Bacombe Hill**, following a path beside the large ditch – look back for a great view – and continue straight on through gates either side of a sunken bridleway to reach the **monument**, **trig point** (257m) and view indicator on **Coombe Hill**. There is a superb panorama. ◄ Just past the monument turn left (south), with a line of bushes to the left and open slope down to

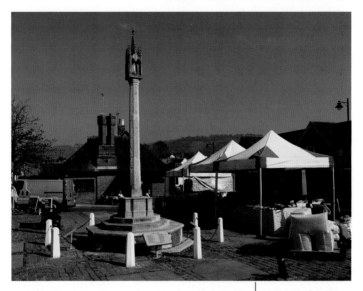

the right; the route is now also following the South Bucks Way. Go left at the fence, then right through a gate and follow a path through the trees to a road with a house opposite. Go right for 100m and then left up the entrance track, before turning right through the gap in the fence. Follow the path southwards through the wood with a field to the left, dogleg right and left through a gap in the wooden fence and follow a rather indistinct path through the trees heading generally south – lookout for the marker posts and signs.

Wendover still holds a weekly market

At a path junction in Goodmerhill Wood (SP 850 051) turn right downhill and keep straight on at the track junction; the South Bucks Way goes left. Continue along the track to a minor road with houses to the left. ▶ Cross straight over to a gate and continue through the field, passing just right of a stand of trees. Go through gates either side of the Chequers driveway, to the left are the twin gatehouses. Continue up alongside the fence on the right to the field corner and go right keeping Maple Wood

It is 5.5km (3½ miles) to Princes Risborough.

Chequers – the Prime Minister's country residence, with the Coombe Hill monument on the skyline

on the left; to the right is **Chequers**, with the monument on Coombe Hill on the skyline.

Turn left through a gate and keep to the left fork, heading west across the field to a gate. Follow the fence on the right downhill slightly and as it bears right, fork left – Cradle Footpath – up the grassy slope of Chequers Knap. Once over the brow go through a gate, turn down to the right for a short way to a junction (for a detour to Great Kimble and Little Kimble continue straight on (see page 119) – this is also the starting point of the North Bucks Way), and turn left down some steps to a gate.

Follow the path generally south-westwards, with **Pulpit Hill** up to the left. Go through gates either side of a crossing track and follow the valley (part of the Grangelands and Pulpit Hill Nature Reserve) gently downhill to a gate. Keep to the bridleway with a house to the right and turn left up the road at **Lower Cadsden**, before forking right to The Plough at Cadsden (water tap – SP 826 045).

Just past the pub turn right up the track and fork left through a gate, keep ahead and start climbing steeply up through Giles Wood to a gate, then on to the signpost on

Looking west across Princes Risborough from Whiteleaf Hill above the Whiteleaf Cross

Whiteleaf Hill and turn left (south); from here there is a great view to the west, with the **Whiteleaf Cross** below. Continue past the Neolithic burial mound, following the level path through the trees, and shortly before the car park (SP 823 035) keep right (straight on) to the road. ▶ Turn right for 10m before going left through the trees and past a gate to a view indicator and seat affording another great view.

Head west down the grassy spur to a gate and down the steps through the trees of Brush Hill Local Nature Reserve. Continue down alongside the fence and turn left along the track (the Icknield Way Riders Route joins from the right) to New Road in Princes Risborough. ▶

At the car park there are information boards for both Whiteleaf Hill and Brush Hill Local Nature Reserves.

There is a map here and anyone wishing to visit the town should turn right and follow the detour directions on pages 114–115.

155

STAGE 4
Princes Risborough to Chinnor

Start	New Road, Princes Risborough (SP 812 031)
Finish	Hill Road just south-east of Chinnor (SP 760 002)
Distance	8.7km (5½ miles); cumulative 37km (23¼ miles)
Time	2½–3 hours
Height gain	210m
Note	For information on maps and facilities en route see West-to-East Stage 9 (page 108).

This short section takes us from Princes Risborough to Chinnor, passing over Lodge Hill with some great views of the Chiltern scarp. At Hempton Wainhill the Ridgeway is joined by the Swan's Way, and both long-distance paths take the same route as far as Watlington. Chinnor, once the site of a large cement works, is now home to a preserved steam railway as well as shops, pubs and accommodation.

Anyone looking for a detour could follow a bit of the Chiltern Way to visit the historic Lacey Green Windmill. Or take a shorter detour to Bledlow, used as the setting for some episodes of the TV series *Midsomer Murders* and *Miss Marple*, and home to the Lions of Bledlow pub as well as picturesque houses and a tranquil waterside garden.

See maps from pages 113–109.

◀ Cross straight over and continue along the track, soon crossing a school access road and head downhill with houses on the right to the A4010 (for Princes Risborough Rail Station go right, fork left along Poppy Road and left along Station Road).

Turn left for 600m and cross over at the traffic island before going right (south-west) along Upper Icknield Way towards Shootacre Corner; it is 6.8km (4¼ miles) to Chinnor. Go straight on at the crossroads and at the brow of the hill head diagonally left across the field, passing under the power lines to a junction. ◀ Go through a gate and follow the path over the Saunderton Tunnel to another gate and head down the field. Go straight on through the gate and scrub before carefully crossing the

The Chiltern Way to the left can be followed to detour to Lacey Green windmill (see page 111).

PUDDING STONE

railway to another gate and follow the enclosed path past the **golf course**.

Go through a gate and continue straight on before bearing left along the gravel driveway. Cross over the road and follow the field edge on the left, keeping close as it turns left to a path junction. Turn right (the path to the south-east heads for Saunderton railway station), still following the left-hand field edge, and keep ahead through two gates. Start climbing steeply up **Lodge Hill**, following the fence and at the top bear right, soon passing a seat with a great view out over Princes Risborough. Continue through a line of mature beech trees and a gate heading north-west – with more great views – before descending through the trees. Keep along the field edge and turn left through a gate in the hedge.

Follow the path across two fields separated by a gate and ignore a crossing bridleway. Go through another gate and cross the minor road diagonally left to a gate; it is 3.2km (2 miles) to Chinnor. Follow the left-hand field

The unusual puddingstone at the junction of New Road and the A4010 in Princes Risborough

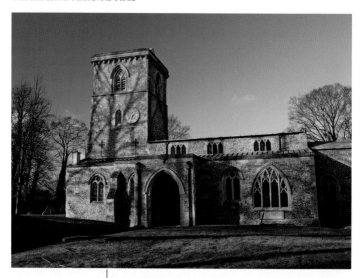

Holy Trinity Church in Bledlow

The track to the right (Swan's Way and Midshires Way) leads to Bledlow and the Lions of Bledlow pub.

Those who wish to visit Chinnor can detour right along the track or at the main road.

boundary; soon the Chiltern Way joins from the left. Keep ahead and turn left through a gate. Bear right, following the right-hand field edge – the Chiltern Way goes right at a stile – and, as the fence bends right, go straight on across the field to a gate and turn left along the track; after 40m a bridleway to the right leads down to **Bledlow**.

Follow the track heading in a general westerly direction for 800m to a junction beside a cottage and turn left, leaving Buckinghamshire and entering Oxfordshire; the Swan's Way now follows the Ridgeway for 13.7km (8½ miles). ◄ Keep right (straight on) at the split; the left fork leads to Berkshire, Buckinghamshire and Oxfordshire Wildlife Trust (BBOWT)'s Chinnor Hill Nature Reserve and Barrows. Head south-west along the fairly level route, keeping to the right at the next split (straight on); the left fork heads steeply up to the Chinnor Hill Nature Reserve car park. Just follow the level track soon passing a house on the left and then a track junction (SP 762 005) and continue past a parking area (SP 760 002) to a road. ◄

STAGE 5

Chinnor to Watlington

Start	Hill Road just south-east of Chinnor (SP 760 002)
Finish	Junction of Ridgeway and Hill Road in Watlington (SU 698 939)
Distance	9.1km (5¾ miles); cumulative 46.1km (29 miles)
Time	2½–3 hours
Height gain	110m
Note	For information on maps and facilities en route see West-to-East Stage 8 (page 100).

Both the Ridgeway and Swan's Way head south-westwards below the steep scarp slope of the Chilterns. We leave behind the old chalk quarries at Chinnor – the large quarry to the left of the Ridgeway has now been designated as a Site of Scientific Interest due to the layers of chalk strata that have been exposed – and later pass under the M40 motorway that slices through the Aston Rowant Nature Reserve before arriving at Watlington.

The town, which is a short way north-west of the Ridgeway, is worth a visit (see pages 98–99), while to the left is Watlington Hill and the White Mark, offering a great view. Detours along the way include Crowell, Kingston Blount and Aston Rowant, as well as Lewknor with its interesting church.

▶ Follow the track south-westwards between fences with glimpses of the old chalk quarries, once part of the cement works – a gate on the left at SU 753 994 gives access to the BBOWT Oakley Hill Nature Reserve – and keep ahead at a track junction; to visit **Crowell** turn right. Go straight over the Kingston Blount road (small parking area at SU 741 986; to visit the village turn right).

Keep ahead (a crossing bridleway (SU 734 981) heads north-west to the B4009 and **Aston Rowant**) and cross straight over the A40; it is now 4.9km (3 miles) to Hill Road in Watlington. Soon a path goes to the left and then there is a sign for a water tap at the building on the left (SU 727 976). The Ridgeway continues straight on towards the M40, later a gate on the left gives access to

See maps from pages 106–101.

*Looking south-west
towards Shirburn Hill*

the northern half of the **Aston Rowant National Nature
Reserve**. Go through the underpass and straight on at the
minor road with parking area (SU 720 968); to the right
is **Lewknor** (see page 102) and left leads to the southern
half of the Aston Rowant National Nature Reserve.

Continue in a south-westerly direction between
hedges and then along the tree-shaded track, with
Shirburn Hill to the left, to reach a junction with a surfaced track – this is the **Oxfordshire Way** (SU 703 945); it
is 8.1km (5 miles) to the A4130 at Nuffield and **Christmas
Common** is 1.6km (1 mile) to the left. Keep ahead to
reach a junction with Hill Road (car park – SU 698 939).
To visit **Watlington** turn right (there is a water tap at White
Mark Farm campsite – SU 697 939); for **Watlington Hill**
and the **White Mark** detour to the left.

STAGE 6

Watlington to Mongewell Park

Start	Junction of Ridgeway and Hill Road in Watlington (SU 698 939)
Finish	The A4130 just north of Mongewell Park (SU 610 881)
Distance	15.2km (9½ miles); cumulative 61.3km (38½ miles)
Time	4¼–5¼ hours
Height gain	330m
Note	For information on maps and facilities en route see West-to-East Stage 7 (page 89).

A fairly hilly section sees the Ridgeway meandering through lovely Chiltern scenery, soon heading south through Swyncombe – home to the peaceful St Botolph's Church – to arrive at Nuffield. A short detour here leads to Nuffield Place, former home of William Morris, the man behind Morris Motors. The last part of the stage sees the Ridgeway following the ancient earthwork of Grim's Ditch westwards to Mongewell.

This stage offers two fairly long detours. The first, to the west of the Ridgeway, is to the historic village of Ewelme, home to the oldest school in the country, while the nearby churchyard is the resting place of *Three Men in a Boat* author Jerome K Jerome. The second option is a visit to the historic riverside town of Wallingford – a great place for an overnight stop.

▶ Continue along the track opposite to reach the B480 next to **Icknield House** and go straight over, following the surfaced track. (There is a parallel permissive path in the field on the left.) Where the surfaced track bends right go straight on past Ridge Farm; the Shakespeare's Way joins from the left and soon turns off to the right. Keep ahead to a minor road and parking area (SU 681 921); it is 5.6km (3½ miles) to the A4130 at Nuffield, and the road to the right leads to **Britwell Salome**.

Cross straight over, follow the hedge-lined track for 300m and turn left (the Swan's Way goes straight on); keep left to pass the old buildings at North Farm. Continue along the edge of the large field and start

See maps from pages 98–90.

St Botolph's Church at Swyncombe

Anyone wanting to visit historic Ewelme can detour right here (see page 95).

climbing up through the trees to a marker post and junction with the Chiltern Way (SU 682 913). ◄ Keep ahead over the brow of the hill and down to a dip before heading up to a gate and minor road; to the left leads to **Cookley Green**. Cross straight over and follow the lane down past The Old Rectory before turning right past St Botolph's Church. Turn left down the track for 500m, with **Swyncombe House** to the left, to a path junction (SU 678 898). (The track continues towards **Ewelme**.)

Go left through a gate and follow the left-hand fence up through the field to pass another gate. Continue up through the trees of Jacob's Tent and follow the field edge on the left before bearing right to follow a track down to some farm buildings. Go left between the buildings, soon passing the weathervane-topped gatehouse at **Ewelme Park**; keep ahead through the gate, following the wide enclosed path. ◄

To the right in the distance are the two tree-crowned tops of the Wittenham Clumps.

Bear left at the junction and head down through the trees before crossing two fields separated by a belt of trees and crossing the **Chiltern Way** – just aim for white marker posts. Keep ahead up through the wood to a gate and the A4130. ▶ Cross diagonally left and turn right along the gravel track, soon passing between a house and garage – the next section crosses a **golf course**, so watch out for flying golf balls. Cross two fairways separated by a belt of trees and continue through more trees, cross a gravel path near the clubhouse and head across two fields separated by a gate to a road in **Nuffield**.

To the left is The Crown at Nuffield and the access road to Nuffield Park (see page 92).

Turn right past the Holy Trinity Church (water tap – SU 667 873) and just after the entrance to the White House turn left. Follow the left-hand edge of the field, continue down through the trees and turn right at the junction. The route now follows **Grim's Ditch** for 5.5km (3½ miles), heading in a westerly direction; on the way keep ahead at a crossing track with a house to the left. There is another water tap here (SU 660 871). Head past Oaken Copse (like many Chiltern woods this is a great place to see blubells in spring) to a minor road (SU 636 875 – Ridgeway Map). ▶ Continue

Both the Swan's Way and Chiltern Way cross here following the lane north-south.

The Crown at Nuffield

Looking west along Grim's Ditch near Cart Gap

straight on along the tree-shaded ridge to cross another minor road at **Cart Gap** and then pass a **trig point** (98m); soon **Wallingford** comes into view.

Go through the gate and cross the **A4074** before turning right and then left through another gate following a path through the trees. Dogleg right and left through a gate and continue parallel with the A4130 to a junction (SU 610 881) and turn left. Anyone wishing to visit Wallingford or Cholsey should turn right through the underpass.

STAGE 7
Mongewell Park to Streatley

Start	The A4130 just north of Mongewell Park (SU 610 881)
Finish	Crossroads on the A329 in Streatley (SU 591 807)
Distance	9.5km (6 miles); cumulative 70.8km (44½ miles)
Time	2½–3 hours
Height gain	60m
Note	For information on maps and facilities en route see West-to-East Stage 6 (page 77).

The Ridgeway leaves behind the Chiltern Hills in favour of the fairly flat terrain close to the River Thames (England's longest river). Call in at North Stoke's church to see some fascinating 14th-century wall paintings, before following the peaceful riverside path. On the way the Ridgeway passes under the twin multi-arched viaducts built to carry Isambard Kingdom Brunel's famous Great Western Railway, with the Thames Path National Trail on the opposite bank. The route heads southwards through South Stoke, home to a picturesque brick and flint pub before arriving at Goring – where the Ridgeway and Thames Path briefly meet – and the neighbouring village of Streatley across the River Thames, home to a youth hostel and a pub. A short detour exploring the riverside town of Goring should not be missed.

▶ Head south along the enclosed bridleway to a lane; a short detour to the right leads to St John's Church.

See maps from pages 85–80.

Follow the lane southwards soon passing between a pond (left) and houses and keep ahead at the junction with Judge's Ride; the buildings to the right are the former **Carmel College** at **Mongewell Park**. Continue straight on, later following a hedge-lined path past the **golf course** (part of Springs Hotel) and then on through **North Stoke**, passing the village hall before turning right along Church Lane; it is 3.6km (2¼ miles) to South Stoke. Go through the churchyard, passing just right of St Mary's Church to a gate, and head across the field to another gate. Follow the enclosed path and then continue through three fields separated by gates before following another enclosed path to

The unusual village hall in North Stoke

a track, with a house to the left. Turn right towards the River Thames and go left, soon passing a WWII pillbox.

The Ridgeway now follows the riverside path for 2km (1¼ miles) passing under the twin multi-arched brick viaducts on the way. ▶ Go through a small gate and turn left along the track heading away from the river. Keep right at the junction and right again (the Swan's Way joins from the left), following the lane through **South Stoke**, passing St Andrew's Church and The Perch and Pike Inn. Keep ahead at the junction and where the road goes left continue straight on across the open field, with the railway to the left.

On the opposite bank is Moulsford.

Continue southwards past some houses and straight over the drive that leads down to the Leatherne Bottel riverside restaurant, soon following a surfaced track with the river down to the right. Go straight on along Cleeve Road and after a short rise, next to Cleevemede on the left, fork right along the enclosed path and then straight on along Thames Road to a T-junction with the B4009 in **Goring**. ▶

Turn right to cross the River Thames, leaving Oxfordshire and entering the adjacent Berkshire village of **Streatley**; to the right is Goring Lock. Go up the High Street (B4009) – a lane on the right (the Thames Path) leads to the Parish Church of St Mary – passing Streatley House to a crossroads with the Bull at Streatley opposite; the **youth hostel** is a short distance to the left. We have now passed the halfway point, having travelled 70.8km (44½ miles) from Ivinghoe Beacon, with 68km (42¼ miles) still to go before reaching Overton Hill.

A short detour visits the interesting church; the village also has some pubs, shops, café and a train station (see page 79).

STAGE 8
Streatley to Bury Down

Start	Crossroads on the A329 in Streatley (SU 591 807)
Finish	Bury Down car park (SU 479 840)
Distance	13.2km (8¼ miles); cumulative 84km (52¾ miles)
Time	3¾–4½ hours
Height gain	265m
Note	For information on maps and facilities en route see West-to-East Stage 5 (page 68).

The Ridgeway now leaves behind the Goring Gap and the River Thames in favour of the rolling contours of the Berkshire Downs with a long ascent up beside Streatley Warren – at the top take a look back for views of the Chilterns. Further on through the stage the views stretch south-west to the North Hampshire Downs some 25km (15½ miles) away before a quick dip under the A34 brings us to Bury Down.

Detours include Aldworth, home to the 'Aldworth Giants' – nine larger than life effigies of the de la Beche family – historic Blewbury, and East Ilsley, once famed for its sheep market.

See maps from pages 73–69.

◄ Turn right along the A329, soon cross over and fork left along the **A417**, before going left along Rectory Road for 2.4km (1½ miles). Fork right along the track past the **parking area** and Ridgeway map (SU 567 812), and follow the track steadily uphill, heading west. At the top, near **Warren Farm**, keep straight on at the junction (SU 549 812); anyone wishing to visit **Aldworth** should turn left along the track (see page 73), with views across Streatley Warren to the Chilterns. Soon a track from Starveall and Aldworth joins from the left. Keep ahead at a crossing byway. ◄ Keep straight on at two crossing routes passing some pine trees, with **Roden Downs** to the left (the route to the north leads to Blewbury).

The track to the right passes Lowbury Hill (186m), site of a Roman temple.

Head downhill and keep left at the split to cross an old railway bridge (to visit **Compton** follow the bridleway to the left at SU 518 823), before heading uphill to pass

Looking north over the Oxfordshire plain towards Didcot Power Station (due to partly close in 2013)

a Ridgeway map and reach a cross track junction; it is 3.8km/2½ miles to Bury Down. Turn right (north-west) along the concrete track (the track to the left heads to Compton – see page 71), which becomes un-surfaced after passing the trees on the left. ▶ Follow the track up over **Several Down**, with gallops on either side, heading towards a mast; shortly before the A34 there is a small memorial on the right (SU 492 833). Drop down to the A34 underpass and follow the broad grassy strip to the car park at **Bury Down** (SU 479 840).

To visit East Ilsley take the next bridleway on the left (SU 503 824) – see page 70.

STAGE 9

Bury Down to the A338
(Wantage/Court Hill Centre)

Start	Bury Down car park (SU 479 840)
Finish	The A338 near Court Hill Centre (SU 394 844)
Distance	9.3km (5¾ miles); cumulative 93.3km (58½ miles)
Time	2½–3 hours
Height gain	100m
Note	For information on maps and facilities en route see West-to-East Stage 4 (page 62).

The Ridgeway continues westwards along the chalk ridge and this short, fairly level section leads us from Bury Down, past the monument to Lord Wantage to the junction with the A338, close to the Court Hill Centre, which offers both food and accommodation. Along the way we catch sight of the Harwell Science and Innovation Campus and Didcot.

Down below the scarp are the picturesque villages of East Hendred, West Hendred and Ardington, while to the south is West Ilsley and Farnborough, where the church has a colourful memorial window to Sir John Betjeman.

See maps from pages 67–62.

A crossing bridleway at (SU 442 849) heads right towards Ardington and just beyond the gate is a memorial to Lady Penelope Betjeman (1910–1986).

◀ Cross straight over the minor road that leads left to West Ilsley and follow the broad grassy track for 2.3km (1½ miles) to a car park and minor road (SU 458 850), passing from Berkshire into Oxfordshire (a crossing bridleway at SU 462 848 heads southwards to **West Ilsley**).

Continue straight on past a trig point on Cuckhamsley Hill (203m) – the gate on the left gives access to **Scutchamer Knob** – and follow the track generally west for 2.8km (1¾ miles). ◀ Later, at some fir trees on the right, fork slightly up to the left (south-west) to pass a **monument** to Lord Wantage and reach a **car park** (SU 418 841). Anyone wishing to visit **Farnborough** can follow a detour to the left.

Cross straight over the B4494, passing another car park; it is 8.2km (5 miles) to Sparsholt Firs. Keep

The sarsen memorial stone to Penelope Betjeman

heading generally westwards, soon a track joins from the left and at the next junction near **Pewit Farm** go left then right. ▶ Continue past White House Farm and then some barns to reach the A338; 600m to the right is the Court Hill Centre (accommodation, barn tea room and water tap).

Straight on heads directly to the Court Hill Centre.

STAGE 10

A338 (Wantage/Court Hill Centre)
to Ashbury Folly

Start	The A338 near Court Hill Centre (SU 394 844)
Finish	Ashbury Folly on the B4000 (SU 273 843)
Distance	13.6km (8½ miles); cumulative 106.9km (67 miles)
Time	3¾–4½ hours
Height gain	180m
Note	For information on maps and facilities en route see West-to-East Stage 3 (page 49).

This next section continues along the crest of the chalk ridge, passing some truly impressive sites. First up is the Iron Age earthworks of Segsbury Camp or Letcombe Castle, then the convoluted contours of the Devil's Punchbowl. After crossing the B4001 at Sparsholt Firs and then passing over Rams Hill we arrive at Whitehorse Hill. Here a short walk past the earthworks of the Iron Age Uffington Castle brings us to the stunning 3000-year-old stylised galloping figure of the Uffington White Horse, looking out over The Manger and the Vale of White Horse. It was Thomas Hughes, author of *Tom Brown's Schooldays*, who wrote of Whitehorse Hill as 'a place that you won't ever forget' and how true that is – it really is a special place. The final stretch passes the magical Wayland's Smithy – a Neolithic Long Barrow – to arrive at Ashbury Folly. To the north, tucked below the steep scarp slope, is the little spring-line village of Ashbury.

There are plenty of detours to the north of the Ridgeway throughout this section, including Letcombe Bassett and Letcombe Regis – at one time famed for their watercress – with historic Wantage beyond, Sparsholt, the famous Blowing Stone, Kingston Lisle, Britchcombe Farm for a summer weekend cream tea, picturesque Woolstone and Compton Beauchamp.

See maps from pages 59–51.

◄ Go right and just before the houses turn left along the track heading west; at Segsbury Farm a track to the right passes through a former Iron Age fort, known as Segsbury Camp or Letcombe Castle. The Ridgeway continues straight on (a stile and path on the right (SU 378 841) gives access to Letcombe Bassett and Letcombe Regis

with Wantage further on – see page 58). Cross a surfaced track and then a minor road at **Gramp's Hill** (both give access to Letcombe Bassett and Letcombe Regis). Shortly on the right are the wonderfully convoluted contours of **Crowhole Bottom** and the **Devil's Punchbowl** (open access land), which can be reached via a path on the right beside an old stile at SU 347 846.

On reaching the **car park** at Sparsholt Firs (SU 343 851) it is 4.8km (3 miles) to Whitehorse Hill. Go straight across the B4001 (the road to the left heads to Lambourn), following a minor road and fork left along the track. ▶ Just after the track on the left to **Hill Barn** there is a water tap (SU 338 854) in memory of Peter Wren, and soon the track makes a short steep descent – there is an alternative path through the bushes on the left – to a junction at Collett Bush (SU 330 858), with **Down Barn** to the left (the track to the right heads down to **Sparsholt**).

Continue north-westwards to a road and parking area (SU 322 862); to the right leads down to the **Blowing Stone** and **Kingston Lisle**. Follow the track up over **Rams**

Heading west with the Devil's Punchbowl over to the right

The road to the right heads down to Sparsholt and Childrey.

Looking south-west from Whitehorse Hill

The bridleway to the south is the Lambourn Valley Way, which passes through picturesque Lambourn.

Hill – a path on the right at SU 308 864 gives access to **Britchcombe Farm** (campsite and summer weekend cream teas) and Uffington – to reach **Whitehorse Hill** (with a **trig point** at 261m). From here a short detour to the right leads to **Uffington Castle**, the impressive **White Horse** and a great view out over Oxfordshire and the Vale of White Horse. ◄ Having admired the views follow the track downhill and ignore two crossing routes (the first track leads northwards to a car park at SU 292 865 and continues down to Woolstone, the second leads to Compton Beauchamp), to reach magical **Wayland's Smithy** on the right and then the B4000 and **car park** (SU 273 843). It is 5.3km (3¼ miles) to Fox Hill, to the right is Ashbury and left heads for Lambourn.

STAGE 11
Ashbury Folly to Ogbourne St George

Start	Ashbury Folly on the B4000 (SU 273 843)
Finish	Junction of the Ridgeway and a minor road (SU 192 746) near Ogbourne St George, or Ogbourne St George village
Distance	17.3km (10¾ miles); cumulative 124.2km (77¾ miles)
Time	4¾–5¾ hours
Height gain	245m
Note	For information on maps and facilities en route see West-to-East Stage 2 (page 37).

The penultimate stage continues south-westwards, crossing the M4 motorway en route for Liddington Hill; a short detour to the Iron Age earthworks of Liddington Castle is well worth it for the extensive views. We then turn south, passing over the highest point on the Ridgeway at 276m, before dropping down to Ogbourne St George, where there is a choice of accommodation and a pub.

Just after leaving Ashbury Folly, a detour to the south leads to Ashdown House, described as the 'perfect doll's house'. Later on, shorter detours include visits to picturesque Bishopstone, where thatched cottages huddle round the duck pond, and Liddington.

▸ Follow the track south-westwards (a crossing path at SU 270 841 gives access to **Ashbury** (right), while left leads to **Ashdown Park** and house – see pages 46–47), to shortly pass some barns where there is a water tap (SU 263 835) on the right; the surfaced track heads north-west down to **Idstone**. Soon the Ridgeway leaves Oxfordshire for Wiltshire and crosses a minor road at **Ridgeway Farm**; to the right heads down to **Bishopstone**. ▸ Just keep to the track as it starts to climb and pass just south of **Charlbury Hill** (253m), before descending to a road and parking area (SU 232 814). Go left down to the crossroads at **Fox Hill** (the crossing road is a former Roman road known as the Ermin Way), continue straight on, passing the entrance to **King Edward's Place** (PGL Liddington), and cross the

See maps from pages 46–38.

For a more picturesque route to the village follow the dry valley at SU 249 823 (see page 44).

Water tap and trough at Idstone barn (there are several water taps along the Ridgeway)

A path to the right heads down to Chiseldon.

It is 9.6km (6 miles) to Barbury Castle, to the right is Ogbourne St George and left is Aldbourne.

bridge over the M4 to reach a staggered crossroads (from here a detour gives access to Liddington – see page 43).

Turn left up the B4192 for 200m and then right, following a track up **Liddington Hill** (over on the right is an old WWII bunker in the trees) to a gate where a short detour leads to **Liddington Castle** (see page 43). Bear left (south) – passing the highest point on the Ridgeway at 276m – and follow the path gently downhill. ◄ Continue straight on along the track, soon passing a stand of beech trees with a seat and a great view west towards Barbury Castle.

Follow the main track and dogleg right (left heads to **Upper Upham** and Aldbourne) then left, and continue southwards, keeping straight on past the trig point on **Whitefield Hill** (261m) to reach a minor road at **Round Hill Downs**. ◄

Follow the lane opposite towards **Chase Woods Farm** and soon fork right (south-south-east) along the track for 1.2km (¾ mile) to a junction beside an old red-brick reservoir. Turn right and then fork left (south-west) following

a track downhill to a house and cross the minor road, which follows a former **Roman Road**. Continue downhill to pass between the abutments of a former railway bridge (the old track bed gives access south to Marlborough and north to Chiseldon), and keep ahead to the A346, from where it is 6.1km (3¾ miles) to Barbury Castle. There is a water tap at the house on the left (SU 198 733). Carefully cross over the road and follow the lane past the thatched cottages of **Southend**, cross the **River Og** and continue along the track to a junction (the byway to the left leads to Ogbourne St Andrew). Turn right to a minor road – to the right is **Ogbourne St George** – and continue straight on for a short way before turning left up the track (SU 192 746), passing a Ridgeway map.

Heading south over Whitefield Hill heading for Ogbourne St George

STAGE 12
Ogbourne St George to Overton Hill (Avebury)

Start	Junction of the Ridgeway and a minor road (SU 192 746) near Ogbourne St George, or Ogbourne St George village
Finish	Overton Hill car park on the A4 (SU 118 680)
Distance	14.6km (9 miles); cumulative 138.8km (86¾ miles)
Time	4–5 hours
Height gain	210m
Note	For information on maps and facilities en route see West-to-East Stage 1 (page 25).

The final section of the Ridgeway starts with a long climb up Smeathe's Ridge to arrive at Barbury Castle, the last of the Iron Age hill forts along the Ridgeway. After admiring the extensive views the route heads south-west over the Marlborough Downs, passing the White Horse figure on Hackpen Hill, before turning south to Overton Hill and the end of the Ridgeway. On the way a short detour leads to the fascinating sarsen-strewn fields of Fyfield Down National Nature Reserve.

The official end itself is rather uninspiring, just a car park beside the rather busy A4: a much more fitting end to the journey along the Ridgeway is to take the option of the alternative finish in Avebury. This 5.2km (3¼ miles) extension takes you past such iconic sites as the West Kennet Long Barrow and Silbury Hill before arriving at the famous Avebury stone circle.

See maps from pages 35–26.

There are plans for new facilities here.

◀ Head uphill and fork left at the split through a gate to continue uphill to a fence on the left, bear right and follow the broad outline of **Smeathe's Ridge** (on the way there is a seat – rest and enjoy the views looking east to the Marlborough Downs). Go through a gate beside **Upper Herdswick Farm** and turn right for 200m, then left through a small gate. ◀ Follow the hedge-lined path and keep straight on past the toilet block and car park at **Barbury Castle Country Park** (SU 156 760), to pass through two gates and reach the earthworks of Barbury Castle.

Take a short detour to see the sarsen-strewn fields at Fyfield Down National Nature Reserve

Go through the centre of the hill fort to the western edge, although a short detour along the ramparts gives some great views (to the north is the former WWII Wroughton Airfield), and follow the track down to a lane. Turn right for 40m and then left up a short rise before following the track to a **car park** (SU 129 747) and minor road, passing three picturesque circular beech copses on the way. ▶ Cross straight over – to the right is Broad Hinton and left is Marlborough, while the gate on the right gives access to the Hackpen Hill **White Horse** – and follow the track over **Hackpen Hill**. ▶ After a dog-leg, where the White Horse Trail forks left, there is a seat with a view west towards the Lansdowne Monument on Cherhill Down.

Continue southwards to reach the car park at **Overton Hill** (SU 118 680), beside the A4 and the end of the Ridgeway. Before heading straight for the finish take a short detour to the left at Overton Down (SU 124 708) to view the unusual sarsen-strewn landscape of Fyfield Down National Nature Reserve.

The White Horse Trail joins from the right (SU 131 752) and gives access to Broad Hinton.

A byway on the right at SU 123 738 leads to Winterbourne Bassett, while a bridleway at SU 125 729 leads to Winterbourne Monkton.

West Kennet Long Barrow – one of the largest Neolithic chambered tombs in Britain

Alternative finish in Avebury

To finish at Avebury follow this 5.2km (3¼ miles) extension that heads past some impressive prehistoric sites. With care, cross straight over the A4 – to the right is **The Sanctuary** – and follow the track south towards **East Kennett**. Cross the River Kennet and just after the junction (to the left is **West Overton**) go right along a path past a house and then right along the lane to another junction. Go left following the lane past Christ Church and keep to the track between the buildings. Go through a gate and turn right to a cross track junction with the White Horse Trail. Turn right and at the next junction cross slightly to the left and follow the tree shaded path to a stile. Follow the left-hand field hedge as it curves left, cross a stile and minor road and follow the track opposite to another stile beside a gate. Continue along the field edge to a large tree; a 400m detour to the left leads to **West Kennett Long Barrow**.

Keep straight on and follow the path as it turns right to cross the Kennet, heading north along the track to the A4. Go left for 30m and then right to cross the road and

The Red Lion in Avebury

go through a gate; now follow a path alongside the River Kennet for 1.3km (¾ mile), passing some small gates and stiles. Over to the left is the unmistakable outline of **Silbury Hill**. Turn right along the A4361 for 40m, then left across the road and through the car park to the far right (north-east) corner. Follow the surfaced path to reach the High Street in **Avebury**. ▶ Turn right (the gate on the right gives access to the henge and stone circle) to finish at The Red Lion.

To the left is St James' Church and the track opposite leads to the Alexander Keiller Museum and Avebury Manor.

APPENDIX A
Route summary tables

Stage	Start	Finish	Distance	Cumulative distance	Time (hrs)	Height gained
West to East						
1	Overton Hill (SU 118 680)	Near Ogbourne St George (SU 192 746)	14.6km (9 miles)	14.6km (9 miles)	4–5	200m
2	Near Ogbourne St George (SU 192 746)	Ashbury Folly (B4000) (SU 273 843)	17.3km (10¾ miles)	31.9km (19¾ miles)	5–6	280m
3	Ashbury Folly (B4000) (SU 273 843)	A338 (Wantage/Court Hill Centre) (SU 394 844)	13.6km (8½ miles)	45.5km (28¼ miles)	3¾–4½	200m
4	A338 (Wantage/Court Hill Centre) (SU 394 844)	Bury Down (SU 479 840)	9.3km (5¾ miles)	54.8km (34 miles)	2½–3	60m
5	Bury Down (SU 479 840)	Streatley (SU 591 807)	13.2km (8¼ miles)	68km (42¼ miles)	3½–4½	140m
6	Streatley (SU 591 807)	A4130 – Mongewell Park (SU 610 881)	9.5km (6 miles)	77.5km (48¼ miles)	2½–3	50m
7	A4130 – Mongewell Park (SU 610 881)	Watlington (SU 698 939)	15.2km (9½ miles)	92.7km (57¾ miles)	4½–5½	420m
8	Watlington (SU 698 939)	Chinnor (SP 760 002)	9.1km (5¾ miles)	101.8km (63½ miles)	2½–3	130m

Stage	Start	Finish	Distance	Cumulative distance	Time (hrs)	Height gained
9	Chinnor (SP 760 002)	Princes Risborough (SP 812 031)	8.7km (5½ miles)	110.5km (69 miles)	2½–3	195m
10	Princes Risborough (SP 812 031)	Wendover (SP 869 078)	10km (6¼ miles)	120.5km (75¼ miles)	3–3¾	350m
11	Wendover (SP 869 078)	Wigginton (SP 934 105)	10km (6¼ miles)	130.5km (81½ miles)	3–3½	255m
12	Wigginton (SP 934 105)	Ivinghoe Beacon (SP 959 168)	8.3km (5¼ miles)	138.8km (86¾ miles)	2½–3	235m

East to West						
Stage	Start	Finish	Distance	Cumulative distance	Time (hrs)	Height gained
1	Ivinghoe Beacon (SP 959 168)	Wigginton (SP 934 105)	8.3km (5¼ miles)	8.3km (5¼ miles)	2½–3	230m
2	Wigginton (SP 934 105)	Wendover (SP 869 078)	10km (6¼ miles)	18.3km (11½ miles)	2¾–3½	160m
3	Wendover (SP 869 078)	Princes Risborough (SP 812 031)	10km (6¼ miles)	28.3km (17¾ miles)	3–3¾	365m
4	Princes Risborough (SP 812 031)	Chinnor (SP 760 002)	8.7km (5½ miles)	37km (23¼ miles)	2½–3	210m

Stage	Start	Finish	Distance	Cumulative distance	Time (hrs)	Height gained
5	Chinnor (SP 760 002)	Watlington (SU 698 939)	9.1km (5¾ miles)	46.1km (29 miles)	2½–3	110m
6	Watlington (SU 698 939)	A4130 – Mongewell Park (SU 610 881)	15.2km (9½ miles)	61.3km (38½ miles)	4¼–5¼	330m
7	A4130 – Mongewell Park (SU 610 881)	Streatley (SU 591 807)	9.5km (6 miles)	70.8km (44½ miles)	2½–3	60m
8	Streatley (SU 591 807)	Bury Down (SU 479 840)	13.2km (8¼ miles)	84km (52¾ miles)	3¾–4½	265m
9	Bury Down (SU 479 840)	A338 (Wantage/Court Hill Centre) (SU 394 844)	9.3km (5¾ miles)	93.3km (58½ miles)	2½–3	100m
10	A338 (Wantage/Court Hill Centre) (SU 394 844)	Ashbury Folly (B4000) (SU 273 843)	13.6km (8½ miles)	106.9km (67 miles)	3¾–4½	180m
11	Ashbury Folly (B4000) (SU 273 843)	Near Ogbourne St George (SU 192 746)	17.3km (10¾ miles)	124.2km (77¾ miles)	4¾–5¾	245m
12	Near Ogbourne St George (SU 192 746)	Overton Hill (SU 118 680)	14.6km (9 miles)	138.8km (86¾ miles)	4–5	210m

APPENDIX B
Useful contact information

Ridgeway National Trail
National Trail Manager – the Ridgeway
National Trails Office, Signal Court, Old Station Way, Eynsham, Oxford, OX29 4TL
01865 810224; www.nationaltrail.co.uk/ridgeway

Tourist information offices

Goring
Community Centre, Station Road, Goring, RG8 9HB
01491 873565; www.goring-on-thames.co.uk

Faringdon
The Corn Exchange, Cornmarket, Faringdon, SN7 7JA
01367 242191; www.faringdontowncouncil.gov.uk

Newbury
The Wharf, Newbury, RG14 5AS
01635 30267; www.visitnewbury.org.uk

Princes Risborough
Tower Court, Horns Lane, Princes Risborough, HP27 0AJ
01844 274795; www.visitbuckinghamshire.org

Swindon
Central Library, Regent Circus, Swindon, SN1 1QG
01793 466454; www.visitwiltshire.co.uk/swindon

Tring
Market House, 99 Akeman Street, Tring, HP23 6AA
01442 823347; www.tring.gov.uk

Wallingford
Town Hall, Market Place, Wallingford, OX10 0EG
01491 826972; www.wallingford.co.uk

Wantage
Vale and Downland Museum & Visitor Centre, 19 Church Street, Wantage OX12 8BL
01235 760176/771447; www.wantage.com

Wendover
The Clock Tower, High Street, Wendover, HP22 6DU
01296 696759; www.wendover-pc.gov.uk/tourism

Public transport information

For train enquiries contact National Rail:
08457 484950
www.nationalrail.co.uk

Traveline is the best resource for checking bus timetables:
0871 2002233
www.traveline.info

Walking holidays

Complete organised packages for the Ridgeway, including accommodation and baggage transfer are available from:

Celtic Trails
www.celtic-trails.com

Contours Walking Holidays
www.contours.co.uk

Discovery Travel
www.discoverytravel.co.uk

Macs Adventure
www.macsadventure.com

Baggage transfer

Some accommodation providers may be willing to transport luggage to your next night's accommodation – ask at the time of booking.

Carrier Bags provides baggage transfer services:
07733 885390
www.ridgewaytransportation.co.uk

Local wildlife trusts

Berkshire, Buckinghamshire and Oxfordshire Wildlife Trust (BBOWT)
01865 775476
www.bbowt.org.uk

Hertfordshire and Middlesex Wildlife Trust
01727 858901
www.hertswildlifetrust.org.uk

Wiltshire Wildlife Trust
01380 725670
www.wiltshirewildlife.org

Animal Rescue (injured animals or birds)

For sick, injured or distressed animals and birds:
RSPCA: 0300 1234 999

Looking west along Grim's Ditch (W–E Stage 7; E–W Stage 6)

Other contacts

Chilterns AONB
01844 355500
www.chilternsaonb.org

Chiltern Society
01494 771250
www.chilternsociety.org.uk

English Heritage
0870 333 1181
www.english-heritage.org.uk

Friends of the Ridgeway
www.ridgewayfriends.org.uk

Long Distance Walkers Association
www.ldwa.org.uk

National Trust
0844 800 1895
www.nationaltrust.org.uk

North Wessex Downs AONB
01488 685440
www.northwessexdowns.org.uk

Ramblers Association
020 7339 8500
www.ramblers.org.uk

APPENDIX C

Facilities near to the Ridgeway

Almost all facilities, whether accommodation, pubs or shops, involve a detour from the Ridgeway. The distances quoted below show those out to the given place name only (so double them if considering a there-and-back detour), and are provided for guidance only, using the shortest route: the actual distance will depend on the route chosen.

Up-to-date information on all facilities along the Ridgeway is available from the National Trail website at www.national trail.co.uk/ridgeway and also in *The Ridgeway National Trail Companion* produced by the National Trail Office.

Stage W–E	Stage E–W	Place	Distance	Shop	Pub/café	Acc	ATM	PO	Bus	Train
1	12	Avebury	2.8km	✓	✓	2			✓	
1	12	Beckhampton	3km		✓				✓	
1	12	East Kennett	0.6km			2			✓	
1	12	West Overton	1km		✓				✓	
1	12	Winterbourne Monkton	3.1km		✓	3			✓	
1	12	Winterbourne Bassett	2.6km		✓				✓	
1	12	Broad Hinton	2.4km		✓				✓	
1	12	Ogbourne St George	1.1km		✓	1, 2, 3			✓	
2	11	Ogbourne St Andrew	1.6km		✓				✓	
2	11	Marlborough	5km	✓	✓	1, 2, 3	✓	✓	✓	
2	11	Aldbourne	5.2km	✓	✓	3		✓	✓	

Stage W-E	Stage E-W	Place	Distance	Shop	Pub/café	Acc	ATM	PO	Bus	Train
2	11	Chiseldon	3.2km	✓	✓	2, 3		✓	✓	
2	11	Liddington	1.8km		✓	3			✓	
2	11	Bishopstone	1.3km		✓	2, 3			✓	
2	11	Ashbury	1.2km		✓	3			✓	
3	10	Uffington	3km		✓	2			✓	
3	10	Woolstone	2km		✓	3			✓	
3	10	Britchcombe Farm (B4507)	0.9km		✓	1				
3	10	Kingston Lisle	1.8km		✓				✓	
3	10	Sparsholt	2.8km		✓	3			✓	
3	10	Sparsholt Down	0.7km			1, 2				
3	10	Sparsholt Firs	On route			1, 2			✓	
3	10	Letcombe Regis	2.6km	✓	✓	2			✓	
3	10	Wantage	5km	✓	✓	2, 3	✓	✓	✓	
3	10	A338 – Court Hill	0.5km		✓	1				
4	9	Chain Hill	4.4km			2				
4	9	Farnborough	2.9km			2			✓	
4	9	Ardington	4.3km	✓	✓	3			✓	

Stage W-E	Stage E-W	Place	Distance	Shop	Pub/café	Acc	ATM	PO	Bus	Train
4	9	West Hendred	4.5km		✓					
4	9	East Hendred	4km	✓	✓	2, 3			✓	
4	9	West Ilsley	2.1km		✓				✓	
5	8	Chilton	2.2km		✓				✓	
5	8	East Ilsley	1.8km		✓	3			✓	
5	8	Compton	2.5km	✓	✓	3		✓	✓	
5	8	Blewbury	3.6km		✓	3		✓	✓	
5	8	Aldworth	1.9km		✓	2				
5	8	Streatley	On route		✓	2, 3			✓	
6	7	Goring	On route	✓	✓	2, 3	✓	✓	✓	✓
6	7	South Stoke	On route		✓	2, 3			✓	
6	7	North Stoke	On route			2, 3			✓	
6	7	Crowmarsh Gifford	1.7km	✓	✓	1, 2			✓	
6	7	Wallingford	1.6km	✓	✓	2, 3	✓	✓	✓	
6	7	Cholsey	3.6km	✓	✓		✓	✓	✓	✓
7	6	Nuffield	On route		✓	2			✓	
7	6	Nettlebed	2.9km		✓	2, 3			✓	

Stage W-E	Stage E-W	Place	Distance	Shop	Pub/café	Acc	ATM	PO	Bus	Train
7	6	Ewelme	4.7km	✓	✓	2				
7	6	Watlington	1km	✓	✓	1, 2, 3	✓	✓	✓	
8	5	Christmas Common	2km		✓					
8	5	Lewknor	0.9km		✓	2			✓	
8	5	Stokenchurch	3.6km	✓	✓	2, 3	✓	✓	✓	
8	5	Aston Rowant	0.6km		✓	2			✓	
8	5	Kingston Blount	1.1km		✓	2, 3			✓	
8	5	Crowell	0.9km		✓				✓	
8	5	Chinnor	0.8km	✓	✓	2	✓	✓	✓	
9	4	Henton	2.3km		✓	3				
9	4	Bledlow	0.9km		✓				✓	
9	4	Saunderton (and Saunderton Lee)	1.2km			2			✓	✓
9	4	Lacey Green/Loosley Row	2km		✓	2			✓	
9	4	Princes Risborough	0.5km	✓	✓	1, 3	✓	✓	✓	✓
10	3	Whiteleaf	0.8km		✓	3				
10	3	Askett	1.2km		✓	2			✓	
10	3	Lower Cadsden	On route		✓	3				

Stage W–E	Stage E–W	Place	Distance	Shop	Pub/café	Acc	ATM	PO	Bus	Train
10	3	Great Kimble	1km		✓				✓	
10	3	Little Kimble	1.6km						✓	✓
10	3	Butlers Cross	0.8km		✓				✓	
10	3	Wendover	On route	✓	✓	2, 3	✓	✓	✓	✓
11	2	Chivery	0.5km			2				
11	2	Tring	1.5km	✓	✓	3	✓	✓	✓	
11	2	Wigginton	0.8km		✓	3			✓	
12	1	Tring Station	On route							✓
12	1	Aldbury	1km	✓	✓	2, 3	✓	✓	✓	
12	1	Pitstone	3.4km	✓	✓				✓	
12	1	Ivinghoe	1.7km		✓	1, 2			✓	

Notes

Accommodation
1 = campsite or hostel; 2 = B&B; 3 = pub with rooms (including hotel)

Bus
Services may be very limited and/or irregular, and most do not operate on Sundays.

Water taps
These can be found at: SU 198 733; SU 263 835 (summer only); SU 338 854; SU 393 849; SU 660 871; SU 667 873; SU 697 939 (when site is open); SU 727 976; SP 826 045

APPENDIX D

Accommodation near to the Ridgeway

Avebury
Avebury Lodge B&B: 01672 539023; www.aveburylodge.co.uk
Manor Farm B&B: 01672 539294; www.manorfarmavebury.com
Silbury Hill View B&B: 01672 539588

Avebury Trusloe
Aveburylife B&B: 01672 539644; www.aveburylife.com

East Kennett
Old Forge B&B: 01672 861686; www.theoldforge-avebury.co.uk

Winterbourne Monkton
New Inn: 01672 539240; www.thenewinn.net

Ogbourne St George
Foxlynch camping and hostel: 01672 841307
Lavender House B&B: 0772 5324869; www.lavenderhousebandb.co.uk
Sanctuary B&B: 01672 841473; www.the-sanctuary.biz
Inn with the Well: 01672 841445; www.theinnwiththewell.co.uk
Parklands Hotel: 01672 841555; www.parklandshoteluk.co.uk

Liddington
The Village Inn: 01793 790314; www.villageinn-liddington.co.uk

Bishopstone
Cheney Thatch B&B: 01793 790508
Prebendal Farm B&B: 01793 790485; www.prebendal.com
Royal Oak: 01793 790481; www.royaloakbishopstone.co.uk

Ashbury
Rose and Crown: 01793 710222; www.roseandcrownatashbury.com

Woolstone
White Horse Inn: 01367 820726; www.whitehorsewoolstone.co.uk

Uffington (B4507)
Britchcombe Farm campsite: 01367 821022

Sparsholt
The Star Inn: 01235 751873; www.thestarsparsholt.co.uk

Sparsholt Down
Down Barn Farm B&B and camping: 01367 820272

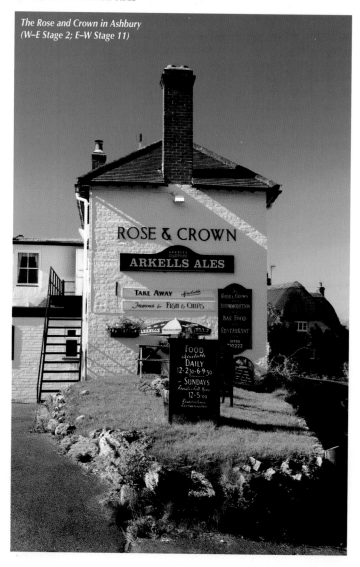

The Rose and Crown in Ashbury
(W–E Stage 2; E–W Stage 11)

Sparsholt Firs
Hill Barn B&B and camping: 01235 751236

Letcombe Regis
Brook Barn B&B: 01235 766502; www.brookbarn.com
9 Croft End B&B: 01235 763694
Quince Cottage B&B: 01235 763652; www.bodenfamily.info

A338
Court Hill Centre hostel and camping: 01235 760253; www.courthill.org.uk

Chain Hill Road (B4494)
Lockinge Kiln Farm B&B: 01235 763308; www.lockingekiln.co.uk

Farnborough
Old Smithy B&B: 01488 638782; www.oldsmithybandb.co.uk

Chilton
North Lodge B&B: 01235 833182; www.chilton-accommodation.co.uk/north-lodge

East Ilsley
Crown and Horns Inn: 01635 281545; www.crownandhorns.com
Swan Hotel: 01635 281238; www.theswaneastilsley.co.uk

The Court Hill Centre near the A338 offers accommodation and a tea room (W–E Stage 3; E–W Stage 10)

Compton
The Compton Swan: 01635 579400

Aldworth
Fieldview Cottage B&B: 01635 578964

Streatley
YHA Streatley: 01491 872278; www.yha.org.uk/hostel/streatley
3 Icknield Cottages B&B: 01491 875152
Linksdown Studio B&B: 01491 873139; www.linksdownbedandbreakfast.co.uk
Stable Cottages B&B: 01491 874408
Bull at Streatley: 01491 872392; www.bullstreatley.com
Swan at Streatley Hotel: 01491 878800; www.swanatstreatley.co.uk

Goring-on-Thames
Melrose Cottage B&B: 01491 873040
Southview B&B: 01491 872184
Whitehouse at Wayland B&B: 01491 873883
The Queens Arms: 01491 872825
The John Barleycorn: 01491 872509; www.thejohnbarleycornpub.co.uk
The Miller of Mansfield: 01491 872829; www.millerofmansfield.com

The Perch and Pike pub at South Stoke
(W–E Stage 6; E–W Stage 7)

South Stoke
Oak Barn B&B: 01491 871872; www.oakbarn.org
The Perch and Pike: 01491 872415; www.perchandpike.co.uk

North Stoke
Briar Cottage B&B: 01491 835833
Springs Hotel: 01491 836687; www.thespringshotel.com

Crowmarsh Gifford
Bridge Villa Camping: 01491 836860; www.bridgevilla.co.uk
Riverside Park Campsite: 01491 835232/01491 577909; www.nexuscommunity.org
Maran Cottage B&B: 01491 839122

Wallingford
52 Blackstone Road B&B: 01491 839339
Little Gables B&B: 01491 837834; www.littlegables.co.uk
George Hotel: 01491 836665; www.peelhotel.com

Nuffield
14 Bradley Road B&B: 01491 641359

Ewelme
Mays Farm B&B: 01491 642056; www.maysfarmewelme.co.uk

Nettlebed
Park Corner Farmhouse B&B: 01491 641450
White Hart Hotel: 01491 641245; www.tmsteaks.co.uk
Somerset B&B: 01491 641710

Watlington
White Mark Farm Campsite: 01491 612295; www.whitemarkfarm.co.uk
Woodgate Orchard Cottage B&B: 01491 612675
Fat Fox Inn: 01491 613040; www.thefatfoxinn.co.uk

Lewknor
Moorcourt Cottage B&B: 01844 351419

Aston Rowant
Tower Cottage B&B: 01844 354676; www.tower-cottage.co.uk
Lambert Arms: 01844 351496; www.bespokehotels.com/lambertarms

Kingston Blount
Lakeside Town Farm B&B: 01844 352152; www.townfarmcottage.co.uk
The Cherry Tree: 01844 355966; www.cherrytreekingstonblount.co.uk

Chinnor
The Croft B&B: 01844 353654
Manor Farm Cottage B&B: 01844 353301; www.manorfarmcottage.info

Magical Wayland's Smithy Neolithic Long Barrow, with a light covering of snow (W–E Stage 3; E–W Stage 10)

Henton
Peacock Inn: 01844 353519; www.peacockcountryinn.co.uk

Loosley Row
Greenhills Garden Apartment B&B: 01844 342409; www.princesrisborough-bedbreakfast.co.uk

Saunderton
Ridgeway Lodge B&B: 01844 345438; www.ridgewaylodge.co.uk
The Chiltern Hotel: 01844 345299; www.the-chiltern.co.uk

Princes Risborough
Brimmers Farm Camping: 01844 346171; www.brimmersfarm.co.uk

Whiteleaf
Red Lion: 01844 344476; www.theredlionwhiteleaf.co.uk

Askett
Solis Ortu B&B: 01844 347777

Cadsden
Plough at Cadsden: 01844 343302; www.plough-at-cadsden.co.uk

Wendover
17 Icknield Close B&B: 01296 583285
17 Orchard Close B&B: 01296 623624
Red Lion Hotel: 01296 622266; www.redlionhotelwendover.co.uk

Wendover Dean
Mayertorne Cottage B&B: 01296 620830; www.mayertorne.co.uk

Chivery
Chivery Dairy B&B: 01296 623065

Wigginton
Greyhound Inn: 01442 824631; www.greyhoundtring.co.uk

Tring
Pendley Manor Hotel: 01442 891891; www.pendley-manor.co.uk

Aldbury
Folly Farm B&B: 01442 851645; www.follyfarmbedandbreakfast.co.uk
Greyhound Inn: 01442 851228; www.greyhoundaldbury.co.uk

Ivinghoe
Brownlow B&B: 01296 668787; www.thebrownlow.com
Silver Birch Campsite: 01296 668348
Town Farm Campsite: 01296 668455; www.townfarmcamping.co.uk

APPENDIX E

Further reading

Burl, Aubrey *Prehistoric Avebury*
(Yale University Press; 2nd Revised edition, 2002)

Carter, Ian; Whitlow Gerry *Red Kites in the Chilterns*
(Chilterns Conservation Board; 2nd edition 2005)

Cleare, John *The Ridgeway*
(Frances Lincoln, 2011)

Dillon, Paddy *The National Trails*
(Cicerone, 2007)

Joslin, Jos (Editor) *The Ridgeway National Trail Companion: A Guide for Walkers, Horse riders and Cyclists to Accommodation, Facilities and Services*
(National Trails Office, 7th edition, 2012)

Leary, Jim; Field, David *The Story of Silbury Hill*
(English Heritage, 2010)

Pevsner, Nikolaus (founding editor) *The Buildings of England*, a series of guides split by county including Wiltshire, Oxfordshire, Berkshire and Buckinghamshire
(Yale University Press)

Pollard, Joshua; Reynolds, Andrew *Avebury: Biography of a Landscape*
(The History Press, 2002)

Quinlan, Ray *The Greater Ridgeway*
(Cicerone, 2003)

Smith, Esther *White Horses of Wiltshire and Uffington*
(Forward Publications, 2004)

A good track heads over Berwick Bassett Down on the way to Hackpen Hill
(W–E Stage 1; E–W Stage 12)

NOTES

NOTES

The leading authority on hillwalking and backpacking for 33 years

Written for hillwalkers by hillwalkers, TGO provides a fresh and vital read for people who share a passion for the great outdoors. Every month, TGO is full of thought-provoking articles, varied and exhilarating routes, expert gear reviews and outstanding photography.

LISTING OF CICERONE GUIDES

BRITISH ISLES CHALLENGES, COLLECTIONS AND ACTIVITIES

The End to End Trail
The Mountains of England and Wales
1 Wales & 2 England
The National Trails
The Relative Hills of Britain
The Ridges of England, Wales and Ireland
The UK Trailwalker's Handbook
The UK's County Tops
Three Peaks, Ten Tors

MOUNTAIN LITERATURE

Unjustifiable Risk?

UK CYCLING

Border Country Cycle Routes
Cycling in the Hebrides
Cycling in the Peak District
Cycling the Pennine Bridleway
Mountain Biking in the Lake District
Mountain Biking in the Yorkshire Dales
Mountain Biking on the South Downs
The C2C Cycle Route
The End to End Cycle Route
The Lancashire Cycleway

SCOTLAND

Backpacker's Britain
Central and Southern Scottish Highlands
Northern Scotland
Ben Nevis and Glen Coe
Great Mountain Days in Scotland
North to the Cape
Not the West Highland Way
Scotland's Best Small Mountains
Scotland's Far West
Scotland's Mountain Ridges
Scrambles in Lochaber
The Ayrshire and Arran Coastal Paths
The Border Country
The Great Glen Way

The Isle of Mull
The Isle of Skye
The Pentland Hills
The Southern Upland Way
The Speyside Way
The West Highland Way
Walking in Scotland's Far North
Walking in the Cairngorms
Walking in the Ochils, Campsie Fells and Lomond Hills
Walking in Torridon
Walking Loch Lomond and the Trossachs
Walking on Harris and Lewis
Walking on Jura, Islay and Colonsay
Walking on Rum and the Small Isles
Walking on the Isle of Arran
Walking on the Orkney and Shetland Isles
Walking on Uist and Barra
Walking the Corbetts
1 South of the Great Glen
Walking the Galloway Hills
Walking the Lowther Hills
Walking the Munros
1 Southern, Central and Western Highlands
2 Northern Highlands and the Cairngorms
Winter Climbs Ben Nevis and Glen Coe
Winter Climbs in the Cairngorms
World Mountain Ranges: Scotland

NORTHERN ENGLAND TRAILS

A Northern Coast to Coast Walk
Backpacker's Britain
Northern England
Hadrian's Wall Path
The Dales Way
The Pennine Way
The Spirit of Hadrian's Wall

NORTH EAST ENGLAND, YORKSHIRE DALES AND PENNINES

Historic Walks in North Yorkshire

South Pennine Walks
St Oswald's Way and St Cuthbert's Way
The Cleveland Way and the Yorkshire Wolds Way
The North York Moors
The Reivers Way
The Teesdale Way
The Yorkshire Dales
North and East
South and West
Walking in County Durham
Walking in Northumberland
Walking in the North Pennines
Walks in Dales Country
Walks in the Yorkshire Dales
Walks on the North York Moors
1 & 2

NORTH WEST ENGLAND AND THE ISLE OF MAN

Historic Walks in Cheshire
Isle of Man Coastal Path
The Isle of Man
The Lune Valley and Howgills
The Ribble Way
Walking in Cumbria's Eden Valley
Walking in Lancashire
Walking in the Forest of Bowland and Pendle
Walking on the West Pennine Moors
Walks in Lancashire Witch Country
Walks in Ribble Country
Walks in Silverdale and Arnside
Walks in the Forest of Bowland

LAKE DISTRICT

Coniston Copper Mines
Great Mountain Days in the Lake District
Lake District Winter Climbs
Lakeland Fellranger
The Central Fells
The Mid-Western Fells
The Near Eastern Fells
The Northern Fells
The North-Western Wells
The Southern Fells

The Robert Louis Stevenson Trail
Tour of the Oisans: The GR54
Tour of the Queyras
Tour of the Vanoise
Trekking in the Vosges and Jura
Vanoise Ski Touring
Walking in Provence
Walking in the Auvergne
Walking in the Cathar Region
Walking in the Cevennes
Walking in the Dordogne
Walking in the Haute Savoie North & South
Walking in the Languedoc
Walking in the Tarentaise and Beaufortain Alps
Walking on Corsica

GERMANY

Germany's Romantic Road
Walking in the Bavarian Alps
Walking in the Harz Mountains
Walking the River Rhine Trail

HIMALAYA

Annapurna
Bhutan
Everest: A Trekker's Guide
Garhwal and Kumaon: A Trekker's and Visitor's Guide
Kangchenjunga: A Trekker's Guide
Langtang with Gosainkund and Helambu: A Trekker's Guide
Manaslu: A Trekker's Guide
The Mount Kailash Trek
Trekking in Ladakh

ICELAND AND GREENLAND

Trekking in Greenland
Walking and Trekking in Iceland

IRELAND

Irish Coastal Walks
The Irish Coast to Coast Walk
The Mountains of Ireland

ITALY

Gran Paradiso
Italy's Sibillini National Park
Shorter Walks in the Dolomites
Through the Italian Alps
Trekking in the Apennines
Trekking in the Dolomites
Via Ferratas of the Italian Dolomites: Vols 1 & 2
Walking in Abruzzo
Walking in Sardinia
Walking in Sicily
Walking in the Central Italian Alps
Walking in the Dolomites
Walking in Tuscany
Walking on the Amalfi Coast
Walking the Italian Lakes

MEDITERRANEAN

Jordan – Walks, Treks, Caves, Climbs and Canyons
The Ala Dag
The High Mountains of Crete
The Mountains of Greece
Treks and Climbs in Wadi Rum, Jordan
Walking in Malta
Western Crete

NORTH AMERICA

British Columbia
The Grand Canyon
The John Muir Trail
The Pacific Crest Trail

SOUTH AMERICA

Aconcagua and the Southern Andes
Torres del Paine

SCANDINAVIA

Walking in Norway

SLOVENIA, CROATIA AND MONTENEGRO

The Julian Alps of Slovenia
The Mountains of Montenegro
Trekking in Slovenia
Walking in Croatia
Walking in the Karavanke

SPAIN AND PORTUGAL

Costa Blanca: West
Mountain Walking in Southern Catalunya
The Mountains of Central Spain
The Northern Caminos
Trekking through Mallorca
Walking in Madeira
Walking in Mallorca
Walking in the Algarve
Walking in the Cordillera Cantabrica
Walking in the Sierra Nevada
Walking on La Gomera and El Hierro
Walking on La Palma
Walking on Tenerife
Walks and Climbs in the Picos de Europa

SWITZERLAND

Alpine Pass Route
Canyoning in the Alps
Central Switzerland
The Bernese Alps
The Swiss Alps
Tour of the Jungfrau Region
Walking in the Valais
Walking in Ticino
Walks in the Engadine

TECHNIQUES

Geocaching in the UK
Indoor Climbing
Lightweight Camping
Map and Compass
Mountain Weather
Moveable Feasts
Outdoor Photography
Polar Exploration
Rock Climbing
Sport Climbing
The Book of the Bivvy
The Hillwalker's Guide to Mountaineering
The Hillwalker's Manual

MINI GUIDES

Avalanche!
Navigating with a GPS
Navigation
Pocket First Aid and Wilderness Medicine
Snow

For full information on all our guides, and to order books and eBooks, visit our website:
www.cicerone.co.uk.

Walking – Trekking – Mountaineering – Climbing – Cycling

Over 40 years, Cicerone have built up an outstanding collection of 300 guides, inspiring all sorts of amazing adventures.

Every guide comes from extensive exploration and research by our expert authors, all with a passion for their subjects. They are frequently praised, endorsed and used by clubs, instructors and outdoor organisations.

All our titles can now be bought as **e-books** and many as iPad and Kindle files and we will continue to make all our guides available for these and many other devices.

Our website shows any **new information** we've received since a book was published. Please do let us know if you find anything has changed, so that we can pass on the latest details. On our **website** you'll also find some great ideas and lots of information, including sample chapters, contents lists, reviews, articles and a photo gallery.

It's easy to keep in touch with what's going on at Cicerone, by getting our monthly **free e-newsletter**, which is full of offers, competitions, up-to-date information and topical articles. You can subscribe on our home page and also follow us on **Facebook** and **Twitter**, as well as our **blog**.

Cicerone – the very best guides for exploring the world.

CICERONE

2 Police Square Milnthorpe Cumbria LA7 7PY
Tel: 015395 62069 info@cicerone.co.uk
www.cicerone.co.uk